Bookbindings

VICTORIA AND ALBERT MUSEUM

Bookbindings

John P. Harthan

Former Keeper of the Library
Victoria and Albert Museum

LONDON
HER MAJESTY'S STATIONERY OFFICE

© Crown copyright 1985
First published 1950
Second edition 1961
Third edition 1985

ISBN 0 11 290226 X

Printed in the UK for HMSO
Dd 696404 C50 2/85

ACKNOWLEDGEMENTS

The second edition of *Bookbindings* appeared as long ago as 1961 and has long been out of print. Inquiries about a re-print or new edition have resulted in this tardy appearance of a third edition. Though based on the 1961 edition it contains much new material, examples of bindings acquired by the V & A in recent years together with new and, one may hope, more up-to-date information on developments in the British bookbinding world at least. This may increase, for a new generation of book-lovers and binders, interest and usefulness in a publication which is no more than an introduction to the historical craft of bookbinding together with a broad survey of the Museum collections.

In earlier editions I was much indebted to the late Mr Arthur Wheen, Keeper of the Library until 1962. In this new edition I must acknowledge with many thanks help received from the present Keeper of the Library, Mr Ronald Lightbown, from the Deputy Keeper, Dr Duncan Haldane, and from Mr Anthony Burton. I much regret that Dr Haldane's magisterial catalogue of the V & A Oriental Bindings, issued at the time of a memorable exhibition earlier this year, appeared too late for inclusion in my Bibliography. Mr John Fuller and Miss Jane Rick (both of the Library) have given invaluable assistance with the illustrations, including the colour plate section which is a new feature in this edition. The photographs of binding techniques were demonstrated by Mr Adrian Passotti and his colleagues in the Museum Bindery and are entirely new in this edition. Finally, I owe many thanks to Mrs Mirjam Foot, Keeper in charge of Bookbindings in the British Library, who generously shared with me her expertise and great knowledge of the bindings in her care as well as those in other libraries. She furthermore kindly read the 1961 edition of my book and suggested valuable improvements and corrections.

John P Harthan

June 1984

Contents

1 Introduction: the development
  of bookbinding design 7

2 Notes 37

3 Select Bibliography 38

4 Black and White Illustrations 41

5 Colour Plates 137

6 Appendix: the technique of
  bookbinding 146

7 Glossary of Technical Terms 152

Vélin Doré

Vieux maître relieur, l'or que tu ciselas
Au dos du livre et dans l'épaisseur de la tranche,
N'a plus, malgré les fers poussés d'une main franche,
La rutilante ardeur de ses premiers éclats.

Les chiffres enlaces que liait l'entrelacs
S'effacent chaque jour de la peau fine et blanche;
À peine si mes yeux peuvent suivre la branche
De lierre que tu fis serpenter sur les plats.

Mais cet ivoire souple et presque diaphane,
Marguerite, Marie, ou peut-être Diane,
De leurs doigts amoureux l'ont jadis caressé;

Et ce vélin pâli que dora Clovis Eve
Évoque, je ne sais pas quel charme passé,
L'âme de leur parfum et l'ombre de leur rêve.

From *Les Trophées* (1893),
by José-Maria de Hérédia (1842–1905).

The development of bookbinding design

In the ancient world books existed only in the form of tablets or rolls of varying length with no pagination or means of ready reference to the text. The need for a simpler form of record led to the development of the Codex, or book form as we know it today, in which the text is written on separate sheets, secured between two boards and bound together at the back. The earliest codices were versions of the Gospels written on papyrus sheets in the monasteries of the Coptic Church in Egypt during the first six centuries AD. Because of the lack of suitable wood for boards a cover had to be made of layers of papyrus stuck together. This was covered in leather and provided with thongs of the same material, used to fasten the book into a kind of parcel. The leather binding was variously decorated with blind tooling (i.e., without gilding), incised lines or pierced appliqué designs having a centre panel filled with a diamond or circular pattern. Of these earliest Coptic bindings only fragments survive, but specimens of the ninth–eleventh centuries show the variety of pattern and decorative motif drawn from the fund of Hellenistic ornament which was the common legacy of the Roman Empire to the medieval world (*Pl.* 1).

Islamic bookbinding had its origin in this highly skilled leathercraft of Christian Syria and Egypt. The Muslim invaders of the seventh century absorbed the craftsmanship and binding methods of the conquered territories, carrying Egyptian skill in leatherwork along North Africa to Europe by way of Sicily and Spain. The technique of Near Eastern binding came to differ radically, both in forwarding and finishing, from that of medieval Europe. Instead of massive, stoutly fastened boards, the oriental bookcover was conceived as a light, wallet-shaped leather casing with a pasteboard foundation. The gatherings of text, lightly sewn, were first fixed at the back of a somewhat wider strip of fabric by means of strong gum; this in turn was glued to the inner spine, much as in a modern publishers' binding. The finishing process differed also both in lay-out and ornament. The most characteristic pattern was symmetrical about a centre medallion of circular or almond shape, having leaf-like pendants and corner-pieces in the form of a quadrant of the medallion. In keeping with the puritanical nature of Islam, the ornament prevalent throughout almost the entire Islamic world until the later Middle Ages was of an austerely abstract type, consisting of interlacing bands, knotwork, intricate geometrical arabesques and various forms of Arabic calligraphy. Characteristic of the Mamluk period in Egypt are the magnificent gold-tooled covers made in the late fourteenth and early fifteenth centuries for the giant-sized Korans used in mosques. The outer cover was frequently decorated with geometric interlace forming twelve-pointed stars on a punched ground, the inner cover with a centre-and-corner design incorporating floral motifs in a manner which anticipates a favourite Persian style of slightly later date (*Pl.* 2–3). ·

With the coming of the fifteenth century, artistic leadership of the Islamic world passed from Egypt and Syria to Persia, chiefly as a result of renewed contact with China. The ancient, severe method of blind-tooling, apt enough for the decoration of religious books, was discarded in favour of delicate techniques agreeable to the splendours, luxury and refined sensuousness of courtly life. Craftsmen at Herat, the capital city of the Timurid dynasty, developed the techniques of exquisite filigree leather, and gilded cut-paper work on a deep blue, painted ground, commonly used to decorate the doublures of bindings. All-over patterns stamped from large metal blocks, designs embossed in thin leather by means of matrices of tough camel hide, landscapes with animals in cut and painted leather, floral arabesques, lotus blossoms, cloud ribbons, coloured and gilded motifs drawn from Greco-Roman, Sassanian and Chinese ornament, combined to produce artistic masterpieces unrivalled in the history of bookbinding (Pl. 4–5).

A further development of the fifteenth century binders of Herat was the technique of miniature painting on papier-mâché boards under lacquer varnish, which was to enjoy such wide popularity in the sixteenth and seventeenth centuries at Tabriz and Isfahan under the Safavid dynasty. The Persian styles were transplanted to Northern India in the sixteenth and to Turkey in the seventeenth century. There they received no significant additions, but shared eventually in the common artistic and economic decay which overtook the entire Islamic civilisation during the eighteenth and nineteenth centuries (Pl. 6–7).

In Christian Europe the Church's connection with book production remained unbroken. As the papyrus plant did not grow outside Egypt, manuscripts of the gospel books and psalters required for church services were written on vellum sheets made from animal skins and covered with wooden boards. A heavy binding of these boards, fastened by clasps, was necessary to keep the vellum from buckling. The sacred books were then covered with gold or silver repoussé plaques, embossed figures, sculptured ivory panels and jewellery; in the twelfth and thirteenth centuries enamel plaques were also used. The richness of ornament applied to these 'treasure bindings' was intended as an act of piety rather than decoration and was generally limited to the Gospels and other liturgical works to be displayed on altar or lectern with reliquaries, plate and other monastic treasures (Pl. 8–9).

Leather was used from a very early date in the West as well as in the East and became the principal material for hand bookbinding. Two techniques were used for its decoration: incised lines, deepened and extended after cutting with a bone or wooden point, known as cuir ciselé (Pl. 10), and cold stamping with small metal dies in the damped leather (Pl. 12). The decorative scheme, which in both techniques was executed in 'blind', followed two basic lay-outs derived from Coptic bindings, one constructed of rectangular panels and the other built on diagonal division. The diagonal pattern, found on Carolingian bindings from the German and Swiss monasteries of Fulda, Freising, and St Gall, reappears in Germany during the fifteenth century. It is seen in a binding from Salzburg which combines free-hand incised lines (cuir ciselé) radiating from large cinquefoils inside diamond-shaped tooled compartments edged with a characteristic bolt-head ornament. This is a tool frequently found on bindings by Ulrich Schreier who worked for Bernhard von Rohr, Prince-Bishop of Salzburg, 1466–82 (*Pl.* 11).[1]

A third late medieval lay-out is the Nuremberg or 'Koberger' binding style (so-called after the printer Anton Koberger on whose books it is often found). In these bindings the centre panel is filled with a repeating pattern of leafy ogival shapes with small diamond-shaped tools in the surrounding border and the book's author or title tooled at the top (*Pl.* 13).

In Spain fine leatherwork was produced in the fourteenth and fifteenth centuries by the Moorish subjects (the mudé-jares, an Arabic word thought to mean 'those who remained') of the Christian kings in the reconquered territories, and also by Jewish craftsmen. The prominent feature in Hispano-Moresque or *mudéjar* bindings is geometrical strapwork formed of double-outline interlacings in rectangular or circular patterns. The background is filled in with roll-produced knot or cable-work designs and other types of Moorish ornament. The example here reproduced is rectangular in design with five ornamental brass bosses on the upper cover; the lower cover has three additional small bosses, probably the mounts for ties or clasps which fastened round the centre boss on the upper cover (*Pl.* 15).

In the fifteenth century new techniques in book production and distribution were evolved to meet the needs of the growth in the number of people who were literate resulting from the expansion of the monastic system, the increasingly important role of the universities, especially the University of Paris, and, most important of all, from the invention in Germany about 1450 of the art of printing from movable types. During this period the book trade was organised on a commercial basis. Printers established themselves in all the great trading cities, particularly on the Rhine and in the

Netherlands, and from there exported books in unbound sheets for sale in the university towns where stationers and booksellers often maintained their own binderies. These early 'trade' bindings, sometimes bearing the name or initials of the binder, bookseller or engraver, while marking the close of exclusive monastic patronage, for many years perpetuated monastic styles of binding. In the fifteenth century particularly, there was a revival of the repeat decoration with small, blind stamps of varied shape depicting fabulous monsters, human figures and purely ornamental motifs such as rosettes and stars characteristic of monastic bindings in the Romanesque period (*Pl.* 12). During this period attention was also given to the decorative treatment of the protective metal studs and cornerpieces frequently affixed to large and heavy books (*Pls.* 13, 18).

As manuscripts and printed books became more numerous the demand for decorative bindings by private individuals also increased. To meet the commercial opportunity the laborious process of stamping by hand with small dies was superseded by the use of large panel stamps of iron or brass which were impressed on the leather in a single operation by means of a handpress. The technique of finishing was further mechanised towards the end of the fifteenth century by the introduction of the role, a cylindrical tool which by rotation impresses an entire ribbon of repeating pattern. These panel stamps and rolls, depicting in blind tooling mainly religious and allegorical figures, frequently adapted from woodcut illustrations, were specially popular in the northern countries – Northern France, the Netherlands, Germany and England – and marked the close of the medieval period of European bookbinding (*Pl.* 14, 16–17).

Materials other than leather were used occasionally to decorate or augment a binding. The embroidered appliqué figure of Christ Crucified on a German antiphoner buckskin cover of *c.*1500 is an unusual example (*Pl.* 18). Forming a more distinct category are the paper woodcut wrapper bindings decorated with woodcut designs and illustrations dating from the late fifteenth and early sixteenth centuries. Most of the few surviving examples were produced in Augsburg, Venice and Ferrara. Of special interest is a possibly unique Flemish example showing the Emperor Charles V on horseback with the Burgundian briquet (a flint-stone producing flames) and an unidentified stationer's mark alongside. The wrapper has been adapted as a cover for a manuscript rent book concerning properties in or near Mons belonging to Jehan de la Croix, with entries covering the years 1552–66 made by his son-in-law Michel de la Houe. The woodcut is similar to others showing Charles V's probable appearance some years earlier around 1540 (*Pl.* 19).

The introduction of gold tooling into Italy was the last and most important development in the technique of European bookbinding during the fifteenth century. Over-all gilding of stamped leather by the application of liquid gold with a brush (*Pl.* 5) had long been practised by Islamic craftsmen, especially in Persia; in Egypt and North Africa, where linear decoration was more usual, designs done in blind were picked out by liquid gilding (*Pl.* 2–3). Both these methods were being used by oriental craftsmen settled in Venice during the mid-fifteenth century. Yet a third, radically different, method, that of gold tooling done by impressing gold leaf on the leather with a heated tool, was known in Morocco as early as 1256 and in Persia by the mid-fourteenth century. This technical innovation of the Moslem world reached Italy by two routes: through Venice shortly after 1450, and by way of Naples about 1475. In North Italy the source of Islamic techniques was the Middle East, with which Venice had trading relations; in the south, the gold-tooled bindings of Naples are in the North African tradition, and probably derive from the Moorish leatherworkers of the Spanish kingdom of Aragon, whose book-loving dynasty were also, between 1443 and 1495, rulers in Naples. The earliest European gold-tooled leather binding yet identified is on a manuscript of Strabo's *Geographia* (now in the Bibliothèque Rochegude, Albi), written at Padua in 1459 for presentation to King René of Anjou.[2]

The influence of Islamic book craft on Italian binding was strongest at Venice, the centre of the book trade in Italy during the later Renaissance; it was thence that decorative patterns and motifs characteristic of oriental bindings, together with the technical processes of gold tooling, entered the general repertory of the Euopean gilder's and binder's craft. Interlaced cable-work and sunken, almond-shaped panels appear commonly on Italian bindings (Pl. 20–21, 25). Gold tooling was at first used in moderation, often in conjunction with blind. The so-called 'Aldine' bindings which are to be found all over north Italy, have simple geometrical patterns of strapwork, or are decorated with rectangular panels of gold fillets having the title or author's name stamped in the middle. The somewhat severe effect is relieved by the use of stylised arabesques and a little trefoil leaf, often called the 'Aldine fleuron' and deriving from manuscript illumination, placed in the angles, sides or at the outer corners of the central rectangle (Pl. 23–23).

The humanist preoccupation with classical antiquity, the inspiration of much Italian Renaissance decorative experiment, found expression in bookbinding through the use of intaglio stamps impressed direct into the leather, giving the appearance of an antique cameo. The best known of these 'cameo' bindings is that showing Apollo (the god of poetry and music) driving the chariot of the sun towards Mount Parnassus, the sacred mountain of the Muses, on which stands the winged horse Pegasus (symbolising fame), the whole design forming a typical humanist conceit. Surrounding this device is a motto in Greek meaning 'Straight not Crooked'. The identity of the owner of this personal *impresa* has been the subject of much speculation. Demetrio Canevari (1559–1625) was for long considered the most probable candidate; later a member of the Farnese family was suggested. Only recently (1975) has it been conclusively proved by Anthony Hobson that these bindings, which date from before 1550, were made for Giovanni Battista Grimaldi (c. 1524–c.1612), a member of a patrician Genoese family with banking interests (Pl. 24).[3]

Italian pre-eminence in the art of bookbinding did not survive the troubled political conditions which marked the first quarter of the sixteenth century, culminating in the sack of Rome by Imperial troops in 1527. The exploitation and development of gold tooling was taken over by the French who became acquainted with the art during the Italian wars of Louis XII and Francis I. Milan, at this time under French occupation, was the centre whence the new style of gold tooling was transmitted to France. A small number of gold-tooled books survive from a French court bindery active between 1507 and 1519, at one time thought to have been situated at Blois, a frequent royal residence in this period, though now firmly assigned to Paris.[4] But it was not until towards the middle of the century, and in particular during the years c.1535–65 that Parisian binderies began the large-scale production of gold-tooled bindings which in decorative effect, beauty of design and skill in execution remain among the highest achievements of the binder's art.

In the 1520s the French book was transformed, in all its aspects, from a Gothic survival into an up-to-date Renaissance ensemble. This was largely due to Geofroy Tory of Bourges (c. 1480–1533) who established himself in Paris, after a journey to Italy, as author, printer, publisher and engraver. He designed two gold-tooled panel stamps for bindings (though he was not, so far as is known, a binder himself), examples of which are now rare. They are very similar in design, each containing Tory's personal device of a cracked vase (thought to symbolise a favourite daughter's death); only the larger panel shows, in addition, the drill or 'toret' of Fate piercing the vase which Tory added in punning allusion to his name. This second panel is found mainly on copies of Tory's printed *Horae* of 1531 and may have been expressly designed for this book. The flowing arabesque design and strange bird forms are Renaissance in feeling but the Gothic cresting which frames the panels looks back to the past (*Pl.* 26).

An important workshop in Paris during the second quarter of the century was that of the 'Pecking Crow' binder, so-called from a feeding bird tool which appears frequently on his books (*Pl.* 27). He was active from some time in the 1530s until at least 1550. The official court binder in this period was Etienne Roffet, but the 'Pecking Crow' binder also worked for Francis I (1515–47). Several of his bindings bear the royal arms as seen on a pair of detached covers in the Museum collection. Another prominent binder was Claude de Piques (c. 1510–75), whose bindery is known also as the *atelier au trèfle* from its extensive use of a shamrock or trefoil tool. Claude de Piques was closely connected with the French court. In documents he is described as *libraire* (bookseller) to the Queen, and *relieur* (binder) to the King. He is known to have been the royal binder from 1559 to 1572 during the reigns of Catherine de' Medici's sons Francis II and Charles IX but the precise year in which he succeeded Etienne Roffet (d.1547), the previous royal binder, is uncertain (*Pl.* 30).

This patronage by royal and other bibliophiles, combined with the use of high quality morocco leather which was imported from the East as an indirect consequence of the Franco-Turkish alliance, greatly stimulated activity in Parisian binderies where professional gilders or *doreurs* of high technical ability showed themselves capable of transferring elaborate arabesque designs from contemporary pattern books into designs for book covers (see cover and note below).★ The theory that gilding or 'finishing' was at this time a craft separate from ordinary binding has been abandoned. Such a division of labour was recognised by an ordinance of 1581 and became customary in the seventeenth century but documentary evidence survives to show that in the mid-sixteenth century forwarding and finishing were both carried out in the same workshop.[5]

The sequence of French styles in the sixteenth century can be followed in the bindings made for the famous collector and bibliophile Jean Grolier, Vicomte d'Aguisy (1479–1565), in 1510 Treasurer of the Duchy of Milan and from 1547–65 Treasurer-General of France. Apart from a group of Italian bindings acquired during his residence in Milan, Grolier's bindings belong to two periods after his return to France, the first from *c.* 1535–47, the second from *c.* 1552–65. The motto *Io. Grolierii et amicorum* is found soon after 1535. He had a number of duplicates in his library and presumably lent his books to friends, though the *et amicorum* formula is not peculiar to him. It was used by other humanists and scholars before, during and after his lifetime; he seems, however, to have been the first to have the motto tooled on his books.[6]

Among the several binders employed by Grolier was Claude de Picques, already mentioned. The earlier Grolier

★ Author's Note: This refers to the cover design
of the 1961 edition of *Bookbindings*, see p. 32.

bindings have strap or ribbon designs, often with fleurons at the corners of the centre panel and the strapwork emphasised by colour, usually black or red. The later period is characterised by elaborate curvilinear interlacings combined with arabesques, an anticipation of the 'fanfare' style of the end of the century. The leaves of the arabesques were often made with azured tools, i.e. tools hatched with parallel lines, suggestive of the conventional technique, of slightly later date, *c.*1600, for rendering in a monochrom engraving the heraldic tincture of blue or azure. During the last ten years of his life Grolier employed an anonymous master, known as his Last Binder, who reverted to designs based on a centre ornament with four corner pieces (*Colour Pl.* 1).

Bindings in the Grolier style were acquired by Thomas Wotton, a well-born Protestant Englishman who lived at Boughton Malherbe, an estate in Kent. Following his illustrious model, Wotton also made use of the *et amicorum* formula and has for this reason been called the English Grolier. The now firmly established Parisian provenance of the Wotton bindings makes it convenient to mention them here. During several visits to Paris between *c.*1545 and 1552 Wotton obtained bindings from three *ateliers* of which the first may have been that of the 'Pecking Crow' binder. The second group of bindings comprises those on which Wotton's quartered coat-of-arms appears, though it is possible that on some bindings these were added later (*Pl.* 28). Also from one of Thomas Wotton's binders probably comes the elaborate strapwork binding with traces of the painted arms of Edward VI of England (*Pl.* 29).

In the royal bindings made for Henry II of France (1547–59) linear decoration is enriched by coats-of-arms, initials and emblematical devices, the latter connected with Henry's mistress, Diane de Poitiers. Interlaced initials, HD for Henry and Diane, and HC for Henry and Catherine de' Medici, his wife, appear on many of these bindings, with three crescent moons interlocked, an allusion to the huntress Diana. Another group of bindings, dating from 1550–65, belonged to the collector 'Maiolus', the latinished name of Thomas Mahieu, secretary to Catherine de' Medici and probably Italian in origin. The *atelier au trèfle* which supplied bindings to Grolier and Henry II is probably the source also of these fine Maioli bindings, though the decoration tends to be richer with punched and gilded backgrounds showing a surface of sprinkled dots as a foil for coloured interlacings and arabesques.

The new styles developed in the latter part of the sixteenth century are known by specific names: 'Lyonese', so-called because it appeared on many books printed at Lyons (though not necessarily bound there, for the style was near-universal in western Europe), with polychrome effects achieved by painting, lacquering and enamelling the geometrical strapwork (*Pl.* 31); 'semis', in which the cover is powdered with repeated impressions of little tools picked out in horizontal, vertical and diagonal rows (*Pl.* 35, 38); 'centre-and-corner', which derived from the Islamic use of sunken panels (*Pl.* 34); and 'fanfare', the most splendid style of all (*Pl.* 36).

The origin of the fanfare style is in the combination of acanthus leaves and strapwork found both on Italian and Grolier bindings, but towards the end of the sixteenth century it underwent a transformation. The tools became smaller and the strapwork was reduced with geometrical precision to a complicated system of oval and circular compartments based mainly on the figure 8. The blank spaces between these whorls of strapwork were tooled with sprays of olive, bay or laurel branches and a profusion of ornamental tools such as winged volutes, fleurons and slender coils of arabesque. The only space left blank was an oval compartment in the centre destined for a coat-of-arms. The back of the book was often without bands and decorated with a continuous spray of foliage. Though predominantly a French style, fanfare bindings of a somewhat coarse vitality are also found in seventeenth-century Italy (*Colour Pl.* 3).

Fanfare bindings are frequently attributed to Nicolas and Clovis Eve, probably father and son, who succeeded Claude de Piques as royal binders in the 1570s; the elder Eve died in 1581, the younger not until 1634. Though not invented by them, the fanfare style became a favourite design for luxury bindings during the Eves' long ascendancy in the late sixteenth and early seventeenth centuries. But the epithet is not contemporary; it dates only from 1829 when the French

Restoration binder Thouvenin revived the style for the decoration of a book called *Fanfares et courvées abbadesques* (a collection of popular songs and customs), published at Chambéry in 1613, which he rebound for the bibliophile Charles Nodier.

Two other styles were in vogue during the Eves' long career. The first, and earlier, was an over-all design of small leafy ovals filled with flowers and other devices with one oval left blank in the centre of the cover. At one time these so-called 'Marguerite' bindings were thought to have belonged to Marguerite de Valois, wife of Henry IV, but in 1920 the binding historian Ludovic Bouland established that many were made for Pietro Duodo (1554–1611), Venetian Ambassador to the French court from 1594–97; they may be identified by the presence of his coat-of-arms, three fleurs de lys on a bend, in the centre oval (*Pl.* 37).[7]

The second style established during the Eves' reign was a semis of alternate fleurs-de-lys and the crowned letter H or L, alluding respectively to Henry IV (1589–1610) and Louis XIII (1610–43) whose arms often appear in the centre of the cover surrounded by the collars of the Orders of St. Michael and St Esprit (*Pl.* 38).

In England, the Netherlands and Germany the old technique of blind-tooled panel stamps survived long into the sixteenth century, with a concession to contemporary taste in the use of Renaissance ornament, medallions and figures. One of the first English binders to use gold tooling worked for Thomas Berthelet, printer to Henry VIII, Edward VI and Mary I; he was described in 1543 as binding 'after the facion of Venice'. Elizabethan bindings, when not in velvet or embroidered (which were the Queen's preferences) are mostly based on the 'centre-and-corner' pattern, deriving from Islamic ornament and popular throughout Europe. The interest of such bindings lies in the correspondence of the contours of the centre panel with the four corner-pieces, the neatness of execution and the use of gold-stippled semis backgrounds to bring lightness into a somewhat formal design. A variant was to replace the centre panel with the arms of the owner of the book. A magnificent example is the full armorial achievement stamp of Gilbert Talbot (1552–

1616), 7th Earl of Shrewsbury, described by G. D. Hobson as 'the finest English armorial of this or any other period'.[8] The Talbot stamp is of considerable technical interest since it is an exact copy of the woodcut armorial which appears on the verso of the title-page. It is possible that the same block was used both for the cut and for the armorial stamp on the cover (*Pl. 35*).

German mid-sixteenth-century bindings are characterised by roll-stamped motifs drawn from textile and Gothic floral ornament, cameos, and portrait panel stamps, often of Luther and other Reformers, sometimes in the surprising company of the ultra-Catholic Emperor Charles V. These stamps were impressed on pigskin, a hard, white leather which could stand the heavy pressure needed to reproduce the engraved metal blocks (*Pl. 32*). Gilding was introduced at Dresden by Jacob Krause, court binder to the Saxon Elector Friedrich August between 1566–85. Closely connected with Krause was Caspar Meuser who worked in the court bindery from 1574–8. Tools of both binders appear on the same books and it is difficult to distinguish their work. Meuser succeeded Krause (d. 1585) as court binder and himself died in 1593. With gold tooling came Renaissance decoration in the Franco-Italian style. The tooling of these Saxon bindings is heavier than that of their French prototypes but richly impressive. The magnificent set of Luther's works bound for the Electoral court in 1583 makes frequent use of the initials FAHZS – for Friedrich August, Herzog zu Sachsen – and the ducal arms (*Colour Pl. 2*).

In Spain the bindings on the numerous grants of nobility ('*cartas de executoris de hidalguía*') made in the late sixteenth century form a distinctive group. Those emanating from Granada are characterised by roll-produced borders and a proliferation of small tools which include birds, stars and the Agnus Dei (*Pl. 33*).

In the seventeenth century the most important innovations in binding design continued to originate in France. Fanfare bindings were increasingly combined with roll-produced borders edged with a line of repeating pattern taken from lace designs similar to those used for cuffs and collars in contemporary costume. The influence of lace and embroidery patterns on binding tools is far more direct in the seventeenth than in the eighteenth century, the period usually associated with bindings *à la dentelle*.

Another decorative motif which made its appearance soon after 1600 was the fan. A design modelled on a partly opened fan filled the corners of a rectangular panel, while two fans, placed back to back, produced a circular ornament or wheel to fill the centre. It is thought that the fan style, a variant on the sixteenth century 'centre-and-corner' pattern, was an Italian innovation. Its use in France was restricted, but in Italy, Germany, Spain and Sweden the fan was a popular motif throughout the seventeenth century, and survived in Scotland as an almost national style into the eighteenth century (*Pl.* 48).

About 1635 the tooling on fanfare bindings began to be executed *au pointillé*, i.e., with dotted instead of solid lines and curves, a development perhaps of the sixteenth-century practice of gauffering gilded book edges with designs and devices picked out in dots. Foliage decoration became smaller and was gradually replaced by less naturalistic ornaments, similar to the fleurons used in typography. The filigree effect of gilded, pointillé decoration as a background for the ribbon interlacings or fillet scaffolding of a fanfare binding was enhanced by the use of red morocco leather which in the seventeenth century began to supersede brown calf. Pointillé bindings are often, though inaccurately, associated with the eponymous binder known as 'le Gascon' who was working in 1622, several years before the style became general. The creators of the finest pointillé bindings have not yet been identified; a number of them incorporated a profile head into their designs, a device also found on two of the three bindings signed by Florimond Badier, one of the best pointillé binders; this is a rare instance of a seventeenth century French binder signing his work (*Pl.* 39). Le Gascon's influence was rather in the direction of a simplified style with fillet frames and large fleurons at the angles, the centre space usually filled by an armorial; this style is represented by the group of bindings formerly but wrongly attributed to the eighteenth-century binder Du Seuil. At the end of the seventeenth century plain bindings with little ornament or gilding, except in the doublures, became, somewhat unexpectedly, a vogue at the court of Louis XIV. Because of their exterior austerity such books were known as 'Jansenist' bindings. They were much favoured by Mme de Maintenon, the King's second, secret wife, and have remained intermittently popular in one form or another, ever since; there is an element of piquant surprise in picking up a plain-looking book and discovering that its embellishment is hidden inside.

In England the somewhat stereotyped 'centre-and-corner' pattern continued in fashion during the reign of James I and Charles I, varied by the occasional use of panel stamps, blocked in gold, for smaller books. During this period bindings embroidered with flowers or animal designs in coloured silks and gold or silver thread became popular. These bindings, the work of professional embroiderers, are among the most charming examples of English seventeenth-century applied art (Pl. 41). At Cambridge, a group of binders active between c. 1610 and 1650 produced modest, restrained work in brown calf, white leather and vellum, often found on the covers of congratulatory verses issued by the University on royal occasions. The bindery at Little Gidding, Huntingdonshire, a religious community established by Nicholas Ferrar in 1626, and which Charles I visited during the dark days of the Civil War, was an off-shoot of this Cambridge School (Pl. 40). After the restoration of the monarchy in 1660 a number of more elaborate inlaid mosaic bindings were made for presentation to royalty and other important personages for which the Cambridge binder John Houlden may have been responsible.

The second half of the century saw the production of some of the most elaborate bindings ever made in England. Though owing something to contemporary Dutch ornament, which strongly influenced English decorative arts after Charles II returned from exile in Holland in 1660, native craftsmen evolved a truly national style which makes this period the Golden Age of English bookbinding. The most characteristic feature of these Restoration bindings is the gilt or painted ornament in the form of a roof or gable placed at the top and bottom of the covers. This national variant of the centre rectangular panel is known as the 'cottage' style; it persisted until the middle of the eighteenth century, particularly on prayer books and almanacks (*Pl.* 44).

In English Restoration binding pointillé technique was much used, as in France, with emphasis on quasi-naturalistic patterns formed of leaves, sprays of bay, various kinds of flowers including the tulip and sweet sultan, and bunches of grapes. Two other types of tool were frequently used; a small, double-handled vase and a miniature scroll aptly described as a 'drawer-handle', though deriving from the Ionic capital. In the application of these motifs great use was made of different coloured leathers, pared very thinly and pasted down on the leather covering of the book: 'onlay' rather than 'inlay' is the correct description of this technique. In less ambitious examples a polychrome effect was obtained by staining the flowers, leaves and strapwork. The leather used was that known as 'turkey', made from goatskin; morocco leather, imported from North Africa, as the name suggests, only became common in England after 1720 (*Colour Pl.* 4).

Many Restoration bindings are associated with the name of Samuel Mearne (1624–83), Royal Binder to Charles II, whose activities also included publishing, printing and bookselling. Mearne is known to have been apprenticed to the bookbinder Jeremy Arnold but he was primarily a successful businessman in the book trade rather than a professional binder. He is likely to have supervised rather than actively participated in the work of the bindery attached to his business, where a number of craftsmen, including the Dutch binder Suckerman, were employed; the latter may have been Mearne's manager in the bindery. There are documented examples of books supplied from the Mearne bindery to the royal chapels between 1662–85 (Mearne's son succeeded him as royal binder), but the expression 'Mearne binding', often applied to any showy late-seventeenth-century English binding, is a general descriptive term rather than a precise attribution. Typical of the Mearne style are the large copies of the Book of Common Prayer decorated with elaborate designs incorporating the drawer-handle motif, scrolls and small urns at the corners of the rectangular centre panels, all tooled in a mixture of gold and blind (*Pl.* 46).

A number of other highly skilled binders were working at the same time as Mearne. The brothers Stephen and Thomas Lewis were active as early as the 1650s. They specialised in vellum bindings with appliqués of red, black and citron coloured leather, and in fore-edge paintings under gold of flowers and a wreath with the motto 'Search the Scriptures John 5.39', signed on some example 'Lewis *fecit*' (*Pl.* 42a–b).

The binder Robert Steel served an apprenticeship to Samuel Mearne from 1668–75 before setting up as a master binder. To his bindery can probably be attributed the sumptuous cottage-style binding reproduced in Plate 45. Steel died about 1710. According to the notes made by the shoemaker-collector John Bagford (d. 1716) on the book-bindings in the Harleian Collection, Robert Steel's work was much in vogue in the early years of the eighteenth century, an opinion confirmed by an entry dated 7 June 1702 in the unpublished account books of the Sotheby family, of Ecton Hall, Northamptonshire: 'Pd off Robt: Steel Bookbinder his bill in full £11-18-6', at that date a considerable sum.[9]

One of the very few seventeenth-century binders, other than the Lewis brothers, to sign his work, was Alexander Cleeve; he is recorded as serving an apprenticeship to John Hardin, a London bookbinder, in 1678. On a fanfare-style binding on a copy of the Book of Common Prayer (published in 1680) he signed the upper and lower covers with 'Cleeve Fecit' (*Pl.* 43).

In Italy magnificent buildings were produced in Rome during the seventeenth century. Often embellished with the coats-of-arms of Popes and Cardinals, or with religious emblems, Roman bindings of the period reflected the baroque opulence characteristic of the city in the Golden Age of the Counter-Reformation. The French fanfare and pointillé styles were much imitated in a manner at once showy and vigorous, but typically Italian is the use of lattice-work or fish-scale ornament in the compartments (*Colour Pl.* 3). This continued to be a prominent feature of Italian binding until well into the eighteenth century and after dentelle borders had replaced the fanfare interlace. At the same time sumptuous bindings in velvet and other fabrics were much in fashion, sometimes further embellished with coloured and embossed foils of tinsel ornament preserved under mica. A speciality of Venetian eighteenth-century binding were the highly decorative paper wrappers printed in colour from woodblocks – a revival, one may think, of the Renaissance wrapper bindings (see p.11). They are usually found on the *raccolte* or congratulatory souvenir volumes of verses recording important events – marriages, convent vows, the election to the office of Doge or Procurator of St Mark's – in the lives of leading Venetian families.

Distinctive national styles appeared in Germany also during the eighteenth century. The 'white libraries' found in several of the great monasteries rebuilt in lavish baroque style after the Thirty Years' War are remarkable examples, still little recognised, of the architectural disposition of massed books. Whole sets of volumes were rebound in vellum (at Ottobeuren), or sometimes (as at Salzburg) merely painted white on the spines to give a uniform effect. The creamy covers and gilt-tooled or calligraphic titles can produce an unforgettable ensemble in their architectural setting; the books are usually in very good condition, showing little sign of use subsequent to their refurbishing: the revival of monasticisim in baroque Germany was architectural and devotional rather than intellectual.

Leather was used in the more traditional manner at Ettal Abbey in Bavaria where an extensive binding programme seems to have been initiated during the reign of Abbot Placidus Seiz (1709–36). Bold floral designs on light brown calf characterise the Ettal books and the name of the chief binder, Brother Gregor Kuen (d. 1737), is preserved in the monastic records. Ettal Abbey was secularised in 1803 and much of its library dispersed. Volumes bearing in the centre of the covers the oval stamp of Abbot Placidus have found their way into a number of foreign libraries (*Pl.* 49).[10]

Materials other than leather were much used in German eighteenth-century bindings. Some very pretty covers in silver and tortoiseshell are found on books of popular devotion. This type of book also appears in so-called 'peasant' bindings of pigskin or parchment, the covers gaily painted with hearts and floral emblems to which are often added pious inscriptions tooled in gold letters. These German 'peasant' bindings form a distinctive group of folk bindings for which there is no parallel in England.

In the first quarter of the eighteenth century a new pattern in English binding was exploited by Elkanah Settle, poet laureate to the city of London. Settle's bindery was occupied between 1703 and 1723 in producing presentation books for noble patrons. He reverted to the rectangular centre panel as a frame for elaborate armorial shields built up out of large, clumsily applied separate tools surrounded by florid mantling (*Pl.* 47). In more dignified taste were the 'Harleian' bindings made by Thomas Elliot for Robert and Edward Harley, the first and second Earls of Oxford, with broad borders made up of one or more rolls, and well-defined lozenge centre ornaments.

In the second half of the eighteenth century bindings of great distinction were produced in Ireland and Scotland. The cities of Dublin and Edinburgh, though subject to parliamentary control from distant Westminster, developed a vigorous cultural life in which architecture, learning and polite society flourished. A minor decorative art such as bookbinding, no less than the splendid squares and terraces, reflects this efflorescence. Irish bindings, though sometimes following English 'cottage' and other styles, achieved a national idiom in the 'white inlay', a diamond-shaped lozenge of inlaid white paper, occasionally leather, which characterises the prayer books and almanacks of the period (*Pl.* 51). In Scotland there were two national styles, the wheel or fan already mentioned (p.20, *Pl.* 48), and a vertical stem down the middle of the cover, with branches, often of holly leaves, sprouting at regular intervals; the latter is sometimes described as the 'herring-bone' pattern. Edinburgh was famed for its schools of medicine and many fine Scottish bindings are found on medical dissertations (*Pl.* 50). James and William Scott were among the leading Edinburgh binders of the late eighteenth century; James Scott, active 1773–90, developed a markedly individual style in which urns and other classical motifs appear.

In London in the 1770s several binders produced designs in the 'Chippendale' or 'Chinese' style (*Pl.* 52–3). These charming rococo bindings, embellished with little figures of

Chinamen, columns, lattice work, fantastic birds and dragons, are in a style which was already out of fashion in the other decorative arts; they illustrate the time-lag often found in binding design. Some are signed by James Bate, a stationer of Cornhill, but the example reproduced in Plate 52 is known to have been executed by Johann Ernst Baumgarten (d. 1782), a German binder who settled in London in 1770.[11]

Towards the end of the century the influence of the neo-classical movement becomes apparent in bookbinding in familiar motifs taken from Sheraton and Hepplewhite furniture (Pl. 54). A bindery and bookshop founded by William Edwards (1722–88) at Halifax, and continued by his sons James, John and Thomas, was responsible for several innovations in decorative binding. While Thomas Edwards continued his father's business in Yorkshire until 1826, his brothers James and John moved to London, where they opened a fashionable bookshop in Pall Mall. James Edwards (1756–1816) patented in 1785 a method of covering books with vellum made transparent by soaking in pearl ash solution and then pressing. Drawings and decoration executed on the under surface were thus protected from dirt and scratching. The painted decoration on 'Halifax' bindings is usually armorial or allegorical, but landscape views are also found, and even townscapes, as in the unusual example depicting the city of Wakefield, Yorkshire, here reproduced together with the allegorical figure of Fame on the lower cover (Pl. 56–7).

Other decorative techniques introduced or used by this resourceful family were concealed fore-edge paintings under gold (visible only when the leaves are splayed out) of country houses and landscapes, and 'Etruscan' bindings, so-called because the calf was stained to imitate the terracotta shades of Greek and Etruscan vases (Pl. 55); marbled end-papers of an individual design are a further characteristic feature. The neatly designed vellum bindings of the Edwards firm, with their delicate gilt borders of various designs – vine or ivy tendrils, Greek frets, and a very common roll of alternate bars and circles, derived from the Doric entablature – matched the elegance of the age and found imitators both at home and abroad.

The leading binder in England at the end of the eighteenth century was Roger Payne (1739–97), a superlative craftsman who is said to have carried out all the binding processes himself, including the cutting of his tools. There is a reminder of Restoration binding in his use of clusters of small tooling, but the over-all distinction of his designs and tooling, and the attention he gave to the back as well as to the covers of his books, had wide influence and brought him many commissions from bibliophiles and collectors. The most notable series of bindings which Payne executed were those belonging to the Rev. Mordaunt Cracherode for whom he designed and cut one of the finest and neatest armorial stamps found in bookbinding (*Pl.* 58a–b, 59).

A group of German binders headed by Baumgarten, already mentioned for his chinoiserie bindings, settled in London in the last quarter of the eighteenth century. The wealth and patronage of the English upper classes provided a powerful economic motive, and these immigrant craftsmen contributed much to the revival of fine binding in England. Prominent among them, in addition to Baumgarten, were L. Staggemeier, Samuel Welcher, Christian Kalthoeber and Charles Meyer. A feature of their work was the occasional revival of earlier styles, anticipating what was to become a common feature of nineteenth-century binding. Staggemeier and Welcher (who worked for a time in partnership), for example, imitated *c.*1800 the early-eighteenth-century style of inlaid bindings *à répétition* popularised by Padeloup-le-Jeune, on a copy of Horace Walpole's *Castle of Ontranto* (*Pl.* 60). Charles Meyer followed Payne's example in filling his panels and borders with small, closely massed tools, but could on occasion produce bolder designs when an indication of royal ownership was required (*Pl.* 61).

French binding in the eighteenth century reaffirmed the creative originality of Parisian craftsmen. Two new styles were introduced, the so-called 'lace' and 'mosaic' bindings. In the former the lace-like border found on seventeenth-century bindings was enlarged until it became the most important single element in the design, often leaving space only for an armorial shield in the centre of the cover. The edges were no longer straight but tooled in a wavy pattern giving a lacy effect currently described as *à la dentelle*, but showing a greater affinity with contemporary metalwork as seen in furniture mounts, balconies, railings and ornamental gates (*Pl.* 62). Of the binders working in this style the most notable were the Derome family and Pierre-Paul Dubuisson. The latter, appointed royal binder to Louis XV in 1758 in succession to Padeloup, was a heraldic designer and gilder rather than a bookbinder who, to meet the demand for 'lace' bindings, made use of bronze plaques. Stamped in a press, instead of being made with separate tools, these block-panels are found often on editions of the *Almanach Royal*, an annual reference book giving details of the French 'Establishment'. Dubuisson's designs, which continued to be used long after his death in 1762, have a boldness which contrasts with the delicacy of hand-tooled bindings *à la dentelle* (*Pl.* 63).

Mosaic bindings, the second major style popularised by French eighteenth-century binders, constitute one of the most luxurious types of book decoration of modern times. The technique was used by Augustin Duseuil (1673–1746), Padeloup-le-Jeune (1685–1758), successively royal binders, Jacques-Antoine Derôme l'Aîné (active 1718–60), and the two Le Monniers, father and son (active 1737–80). The style was a development of inlaid bindings, but resembled marquetry rather than mosaic, being characterised by large onlays of citron-yellow, red and green leather combined in massive *compartiments* to form elaborate scroll and floral shapes. A variant was the revival of the 'centre-and-corner' motif of earlier centuries in designs of virtuoso brilliance (*Colour Pl.* 5).

In the reign of Louis XVI (1774–94) there was a return to more sober bindings, inspired, for the first time, by English models. Fashionable anglophilia had already substituted 'le jardin anglais' for the formal parterres and vistas of the Le Nôtre school; now English bindings of tasteful simplicity became the accepted mode in the last years of the old monarchy. The Revolution confirmed this trend. During the Directoire and early Empire period, Bradel, Tessier, the elder Bozerian and other contemporary binders confined elaborate tooling mainly to the backs of their books, the cover decoration being relatively restrained and restricted, for the most part, to borders of palmetteos (the Greek anthemion ornament), lyres, chain-patterns and vine leaves, with sometimes the incorporation of now fashionable Egyptian motifs. Under Napoleon I there was a partial return to ostentatious bindings but it was not until the Bourbon Restoration in 1814 that the revival of French binding got under way.

Early Restoration bindings are Neo-Classical rather than Romantic in style, identifiable mainly by the Bourbon lilies which replaced the Napoleonic eagles (Pl. 64).[12] But soon there began a period of eclecticism with much borrowing of ornamental motifs from the Middle Ages, the Renaissance and later epochs. Blind stamping in low relief, little used since the late medieval panel-stamps, was revived to become a characteristic feature of Romantic bindings (Pl. 66–7). A triumvirate of binders – Purgold, Simier and Thouvenin – dominated the period 1814–30. Their successor in the reign of Louis-Philippe (1830–48) was Bauzonnet, a binder with a masterly feeling for elegant designs made up of simple fillet-patterns.

The cult of medievalism in the Romantic age found expression in bookbinding in the charming 'cathedral' (à la cathédrale) style which popularised motifs simulating Gothic architecture. In some examples, such as the English binding reproduced in Pl. 65, an entire cathedral front, even if much stylised, was transferred on to a book cover. In continental examples, the combination of Neo-Classical and Gothic elements is found in the massive border, with its prominent Greek anthemion·motif, which surrounds the Gothic rose-window in the centre, on a signed binding by Johann Jacob Selencka (Colour Pl. 6). This is one of a series of magnificent bindings of musical scores, now sadly dispersed, made by Selencka for the ducal court of Brunswick in the 1820s. He began working there, as a binder-apprentice from Hochheim in 1824, but appears never to have received a court appointment and later moved to Wiesbaden.

With Selencka we reach the nineteenth century when, almost for the first time, it became the custom rather than the exception for binders to sign their work at the bottom of the cover or spine, or by inserting a binder's ticket on a fly-leaf. Patrons hitherto seem to have been unwilling to see their books 'disfigured' by binders' tickets, or so Charles Ramsden surmised when trying to account for the difficulty of attributing many English bindings of excellent quality to specific binders in the period 1780–1810.[13] The increasing frequency with which binders signed their work in the early nineteenth century and onwards provides a long list of names. Among the most notable in France, in addition to those already mentioned, were Vogel, Trautz and Koehler; in England, Staggemeier, Hering, Lewis and Bedford, and many more, were active in the first half of the century.

The general adoption in England during the 1840s of two technical innovations changed the whole status of binding craft. The first was the use of cloth instead of leather (a practice begun by the publisher William Pickering in the 1820s); the second, the new technique of trade bindings whereby covers and printed sheets were prepared independently by machinery and glued together instead of being sewn by hand in the traditional binding technique. An increased demand for books, following the educational and social reforms of the nineteenth century, was met by the exploitation of these cheap publishers' bindings. A distinction between 'fine' and 'trade' bindings resulted which for a time accentuated the decline in standards of binding design.

'Fine' binding continued to be dominated by the historicist approach in which earlier styles of decoration were revived but given what is now seen as a marked period look. A sparkling Spanish example in the 'Second Rococo' manner, found on a modest guide book, continues a style found often in French bindings during the reign of Louis Philippe (Pl. 66,68). From a later period comes the witty reinterpretation, in an unmistakable 'Nineties' guise, of the 'fan' pattern on a binding made by Salvator David, (active 1890–1929), for Louis Legrand's Cours de danse fin de siècle of 1895 (Pl. 69).

Towards the end of the century the situation changed radically as new concepts of binding design were developed by Henri Marius–Michel (1821–90) and his son Henri-François-Victor (1846–1925) who jointly set up a bindery in Paris in 1876. Father and son collaborated as binders, creative designers and writers on the history of their craft. The younger Marius-Michel was totally out of sympathy with the school of Trautz-Bauzonnet, Chambolle-Duru and other 'retrospective binders' who produced for wealthy bibliophiles superbly executed covers imitative of former styles. Instead he developed the concept of 'original binding', in which a connection is established between contents and covers of a book expressive of the skill and personal approach of the binder. Hitherto, the decoration of covers had seldom been deliberately related to the book's content, although sometimes, especially on publishers' cloth bindings, a random illustration from inside might be copied directly as an 'illustrative' binding.

Two types of design were characteristic of the Marius-Michel bindery: naturalistic floral patterns, and an imaginative use of incised and embossed leather, the latter much copied in England in the designs, for example, of Mary Houston and Alice Shepherd (*Pl.* 72–3). In the Paris Universal Exhibition of 1876 the Marius-Michel firm received a medal for a book of which somebody observed 'This is art not binding', a remark widely quoted at the time, which anticipated twentieth-century attitudes. The influence of the Marius–Michel *renovatio* in binding design is seen in the work of several contemporary binderies, especially that of another family firm, the Canape bindery, founded in 1865 by J. Canape and taken over by his son Georges Canape in 1894 (*Pl.* 70).

In England a comparable renewal of creative binding was brought about by Thomas J. Cobden-Sanderson (1840–1922), a pupil of William Morris, who has been called the father of modern English binding. A lawyer by profession, he took up binding only in middle age. His active career as a practising binder was short, lasting from 1884 until 1893. But in introducing a new style of design, by cutting his own tools and carrying out all the forwarding and finishing processes himself Cobden-Sanderson established a tradition which is still very much alive in British bookbinding (*Pl.* 74). Like Marius-Michel he made much use of floral motifs in his designs, although these tended to be more stylised. In 1893 Cobden-Sanderson established the Doves Press Bindery (active until 1921) for which he designed bindings though no longer executing them himself; the chief finisher at the Doves

Bindery was Charles McLeish. Cobden-Sanderson's influence was profound and lasting. It may be seen in the impeccable bindings of the little-known Charles Elsden Gladstone, R.N., (d.1919) who, following Cobden-Sanderson's example, took up binding later in life, after a naval career (*Pl.* 75). Best-known among Cobden-Sanderson's followers were Douglas Cockerell (1870–1945), at one time an apprentice in the Doves Bindery, and Sarah T. Prideaux (*Pl.* 76).

The revival of binding craft in England in the early twentieth century was encouraged by the superlative designs of Charles Ricketts (*Pl.* 81), founder of the Vale Press but not himself a binder, and the work of the Guild of Women Binders. The latter was founded by Frank Karslake, an antiquarian bookseller, partly as a counterpart to the Hampstead Bindery, which was confined to men, and partly to encourage and co-ordinate the role of women in bookbinding. Between 1898 and 1904 a considerable number of bindings, of varying quality, were produced in which the current Art Nouveau idiom is often manifest. The best examples were the bindings of Constance Karslake and Florence de Rheims (*Pl.* 71).

Revitalising as was the work of Marius-Michel and Cobden-Sanderson in introducing new naturalistic and expressive designs, it should not be regarded as demoting the retrospective binders to the role of mere pasticheurs. To provide a binding in the style of the period of the book it encloses may sometimes be a legitimate aim if the original binding has disintegrated or was never made. Nineteenth-century connoisseurs and bibliophiles often preferred chronologically appropriate covers for their books, as already noted in the case of a seventeenth-century book bound in 1829 by Thouvenin in the fanfare style for the collector Charles Nodier. Technically, the work of the retrospective binders was usually of the highest quality. Bauzonnet (1788–1879) was known as the *grand maître des filets*. His partner and successor Trautz (1808–79) specialised in all-over strapwork designs in multiple fillets, based on the Grolier style, which the collector Beraldi, writing in 1895, described as the true nineteenth-century style in bookbinding. The same approach is found in the books produced by the firm of Chambolle-Duru who produced modern versions of the Duodo bindings of the 1590s and other historical styles. Henri Marius-Michel the elder, it is worth recording, worked for a time in the Chambolle-Duru house. In England the firms of Zaehnsdorf, Rivière, Sangorsky and Sutcliffe, produced similar 'trade' or commercial bindings of high technical excellence which meticulously re-created many traditional designs.

The Marius-Michel style, of which Cobden-Sanderson bindings may be considered an English equivalent, reached its zenith in the Paris Universal Exhibition of 1900, a period when floral motifs were a prominent feature in the current Art Nouveau movement. It remained influential for a quarter of a century until replaced, almost overnight, by a totally new style introduced by Pierre Legrain. A Parisian cabinet-maker by training, Legrain began designing book covers for the collector Jacques Doucet in the years 1917–19. Doucet had sold his collection of eighteenth-century art objects in 1912 and turned uncompromisingly towards the Modern Movement. Legrain followed his example by applying to binding design the contemporary idioms of cubist and abstract art, an innovation which gave a new direction to French bookbinding. The 1925 Paris *Exposition des Arts Décoratifs* (whence the term 'Art Deco' derives) saw the triumph of the new style which superseded, and made suddenly old-fashioned, the decorative, floral bindings of the Marius-Michel school (*Pl.* 82).

Among Legrain's followers were his son-in-law Jacques Anthoine-Legrain, Georges Cretté, Henri Kieffer, Henri Creuzevault, Paul Bonet and Rose Adler. These were among the names which dominated French bookbindings during the 1930s and the immediate post-war period. Bonet's bravura colour sense, highly inventive *rayonnant* designs of massed fillets, and sculptured bindings, achieved great renown and influence (*Colour Pl.* 7). Henri Creuzevault, publisher as well as binder, produced many striking designs such as the apposite 'zebra' binding for Picasso's beast etchings to accompany texts of Buffon (*Pl.* 84). Rose Adler, a distinguished woman binder much influenced by Legrain, specialised in non-figurative forms and a quieter tonal range. Unlike some of her more flamboyant Parisian contemporaries, she never lost sight of the primary function of binding as a protective cover to a book (*Pl.* 83).

The founding of the *Société de la Reliure Originale* in 1946 marked the consolidation of the French school of creative binding and the integration of avant-garde motifs in painting and the graphic arts into binding design. A leading figure in Parisian binding in the post-war period has been Pierre-Lucien Martin (b. 1913). His designs are distinguished by an almost geometrical sense of logic, three-dimensional illusionist effects, inventive use of lettering (a practice pioneered by Legrain) and a relatively muted, harmonious colour range in his leathers in contrast to the pyrotechnic effects of Bonet. A further aspect of his work is that he binds only books written by contemporary authors (*Pl.* 85).

In England, the Cobden-Sanderson tradition was continued in the period between two wars by several notable teacher-binders. These included William F. Matthews (1898–1976), who taught at the Central School of Art (*Pl.* 77), Roger Powell (b. 1896), who studied under Douglas Cockerell (*Pl.* 87), and Sydney M. Cockerell (b. 1906) who joined his father in 1924 in a family business reminiscent of that of Marius-Michel *père et fils* (*Pl.* 86). Attention must also be given to some distinguished women binders in addition to those already mentioned as being active in the early years of the century. The bindings of Madeline Kohn (d. 1940) and Sybil Pye (d. 1958) are in a style which we now recognise as typical Art Deco (*Pl.* 78–9).

Another distinct group of noteworthy bindings comprises the books produced by the Gregynog Press, a private press established in 1922 at Newtown, Montgomeryshire, by two sisters, Miss Margaret and Miss Gwendolyn Davies, who did much to encourage fine printing in their native Wales. Using designs produced by prominent artists of the time, including Blair Hughes-Stanton, Paul Nash and Robert Ashwin Maynard, then Controller of the press, many of the Gregynog bindings were executed by George Fisher (d. 1970), himself also a designer (*Pl.* 80).

A decisive, perhaps the most important single contribution to mid-century British bookbinding was made by Edgar

Mansfield (b. 1907) whose work has been seminal in establishing the principles of creative design by relating contents and covers of his books in expressive rather than merely decorative bindings (*Pl.* 88). His influence has been strong among members of the Guild of Contemporary Bookbinders, founded in 1955 and reconstituted under the name Designer Bookbinders in 1968. This society, which may be regarded as the British parallel to the *Société de la Reliure Originale* in France, brought together a group of progressive binders with the common aim of breaking away from traditional forms and establishing new standards of design and execution which could bear comparison with those of the other applied arts and with the work of contemporary binders in France.

In assessing the work of twentieth-century French and English bookbinders an important difference in workshop procedures should be kept in mind. Paul Bonet, in his own words, 'created' but did not 'produce' bindings: that is to say, he was an artist-designer but not a practising binder although he made a close study of gilding. His designs were executed by professional forwarders and gilders. The same procedure has been followed in the bindings of Pierre Martin. This division of labour, whereby original bindings result from close collaboration between artist, forwarder, finisher and gilder, is a peculiarly French phenomenon. It is reminiscent of the medieval system in which groups of specialised craftsmen were organised in workshops under a *chef d'atelier* to produce the illuminated manuscripts which are among the glories of French Gothic art.

Very different is the English tradition in which all the processes of design, forwarding and finishing are carried out by a single binder working often in the isolation of his or her own workshop. This practice goes back to the Arts and Crafts Movement (if not to Roger Payne and even earlier), to William Morris's creed of sound craftsmanship and the concept of the 'whole book', and to the tradition established by Cobden-Sanderson.

The variety and versatility of contemporary British bookbinding has been recognised in several important exhibitions mounted during the 1970s. To limit examples to the work of the older generation of binders reproduced here in the plate section one may cite the integration of forwarding and finishing characteristic of Roger Powell (*Pl.* 87), Sydney M. Cockerell's toned vellum bindings with gold and black calligraphic embellishment (*Pl.* 86), the emphatic tactile designs of Edgar Mansfield (*Pl.* 88), Elizabeth Greenhill's 'cloud' bindings, (*Pl.* 90), Ivor Robinson's linear clarity (*Pl.* 91), the angular abstract designs of Sally Lou Smith (*Colour Pl.* 8) and the painterly technique, feathered onlays and marbled effects of Philip Smith (*Pl.* 89).

Appreciation and study of fine bindings today depends less on the minute investigation and comparison of binders' tools, essential work for establishing historical sequence and workshop attributions for the bindings of earlier centuries, but rather on a knowledge of the personal style and technique of the designer-executant. From being a minor decorative applied art, patronised by royalty, aristocrats and bibliophiles, bookbinding has developed in the twentieth century into an expressive art-form in its own right. The books selected by the creative binder are regarded as three-dimensional objects with the different parts – text, typography, illustrations and binding (the latter through all stages from sewing to finishing) – clearly related and conceived as an integrated whole. This is not always discernible in two-dimensional photographs; a design extending across both covers and the spine can be seen, but not the carry-over into the doublures.

This radical, ambitious approach has its dangers: bindings may acquire the status of cult-objects and collectors' pieces, akin to the 'treasure bindings', studded with jewels and inlaid with gold and ivory plaques, found on the ceremonial service-books of the medieval church. The artist-binder can never attain to the autonomy of the painter or sculptor since he must work always with his author and with sensitive regard to the text which he is enclosing within an appropriate design. But the domain of bookbinding is so extensive that there is room for every type of work. The multivalent messages and visual variety conveyed by much contemporary bookbinding are signs of vitality which makes the future hopeful.

Notes

1 Laurin, G., 'Der Salzburger Einbandstil Ulrich Shreiers', in *Gutenberg-Jahrbuch* (1960), pp. 371–8, and 'Die Lederschnittbände des Salzburger Illuminators Ulrich Schreier für den Erzbischof Bernhard von Rohr', in *Archiv für die Geschichte des Buchwesens*, v, 1963, pp. 743–75.

2 Hobson, A.R.A., 'Two Renaissance Bindings', in *The Book Collector*, vii, 1958, pp. 265–8.

3 Hobson, A.R.A., *Apollo and Pegasus: an Enquiry into the Formation and Dispersal of a Renaissance Library*, Amsterdam, 1975.

4 Nixon, H.M., *Sixteenth-Century Gold-Tooled Bookbindings in the Pierpont Morgan Library*, New York, 1971, pp. 9–12.

5 Michon, L.M., *La reliure française*, Paris, 1951, pp. 64–5.

6 Hobson, G.D., '*Et Amicorum*', in *The Library*, 5th ser., iv, 1949, pp. 87–99.

7 Bouland, L., 'Livres aux armes de Pierre Duodo, vénétien, et non pas de Marguerite de Valois', in *Bulletin du Bibliophile*, 1920, pp. 66–80.

8 Hobson, G.D., *The Times Literary Supplement*, 14 September 1940, p. 476.

9 MSS, Notebooks compiled by James Sotheby (1655–1720) and his descendants dealing with property and recording purchases of works of art at Ecton Hall, Northampton. Account Book of James Sotheby 2nd, 1701–4, 7 June 1702, Victoria and Albert Museum Library, Manuscript Collections Box 86, KK, Box 1, L.2715–1955.)

10 Brunner, W., 'Der Ettaler Bucheinband, vornehmlich im 18. Jahrhundert', in *Sankt Wiborada*, ii, 1934, pp. 32–46.

11 Nixon, H.M., 'Baumgartner's Will', in *Festschrift Ernst Kyriss*, Stuttgart, 1961, pp. 397–401.

12 Boisier-Astier (C.), 'A French bookbinder in London. Auguste-Marie de Caumont', in *The Book Collector*, vol. 30, pp. 182–195 (1981).

13 Ramsden, C., *London Bookbinders, 1780–1840*, London, 1956, p. 10.

Select bibliography

A General Works

1 ARNOLD, SIR T.W., and GROHMANN, A., *The Islamic Book*, Paris, 1929.

2 BERALDI, H., *La reliure du XIXe siècle*, 4 vols, Paris, 1895–97.

3 CRAIG, M., *Irish bookbindings, 1600–1800*, London, 1954.

4 CRAUZAT, E. DE, *La reliure française de 1900; à 1925*, 2 vols, Paris, 1932.

5 DE MARINIS, T., *La legature artistica in Italia nei secoli XV e XVI*, 3 vols, Florence, 1960.

6 DEVAUCHELLE, R., *La reliure en France*, 3 vols, Paris, 1959–61.

7 DEVAUX, Y., *Dix siècles de reliure*, Paris, 1977.

8 DIEHL, E., *Bookbinding: its background and techniques*, 2 vols, New York, 1946.

9 HELWIG, H., *Handbuch der Einbandkunde*, 3 vols, Hamburg, 1953–55.

10 HOBSON, A.R.A., *Apollo and Pegasus: an Enquiry into the formation and dispersal of a Renaissance Library* [*Formed by Giovanni Battista Grimaldi, patron of the 'Canevari binder'*], Amsterdam, 1975.

11 HOBSON, G.D., *Maioli, Canevari and others*, London, 1926.

12 HOBSON, G.D., *English binding before 1550*, Cambridge, 1929.

13 HOBSON, G.D., *Les reliures à la fanfare*. 2nd ed., London, 1970.

14 KYRISS, E., *Verzierte gotische Einbände im alten deutschen Sprachgebiet*, 4 vols, Stuttgart, 1951–58.

15 LOUBIER, H., *Der Bucheinband*, 2nd ed., Leipzig, 1926.

16 LOUDON, J.H., *James Scott and William Scott, bookbinders of Edinburgh*, London, 1979.

17 MACLEAN, R., *Victorian publishers' bookbindings in cloth and leather*, London, 1974.

18 MAGGS BROS, LTD., *Bookbindings in Great Britain. Sixteenth to the Twentieth Century* (Catalogue 996), London, 1975.

19 MANSFIELD, E., *Modern design in bookbindings . . . and the technique of fine binding*, London, 1966.

20 MARÇAIS, G. and POINSSOT, L., *Objets Kairouannais, IXe au XIIIe siècle: reliures* (Direction des Antiquités et Arts, Tunis, Notes et Documents, Vol. XI, Pt. 1), Tunis and Paris, 1948.

21 MICHEL, M., *La reliure française*, Paris, 1880.

22 MICHON, L.M., *La reliure française*, Paris, 1951.

23 MICHON, L.M., *Les reliures mosaïquées du XVIIIe siècle*, Paris, 1956.

24 NIXON, H.M., *Five centuries of English bookbinding* [Collected articles from *The Book Collector*], London, 1978.

25 OLDHAM, J.B., *English blind-*

stamped bindings, Cambridge, 1952.
26 OLDHAM, J.B., *Blind panels of English binders*, Cambridge, 1958.
27 RAMSDEN, C., *French bookbinders, 1789–1940*, London, 1950.
28 RAMSDEN, C., *Bookbinders, of the United Kingdom (outside London), 1780–1840*, London, 1954.
29 RAMSDEN, C., *London bookbinders, 1780–1940*, London, 1956.
30 SARRE, F., *Islamische Bucheinband*, Berlin, 1923.
31 SMITH, P., *New directions in bookbinding*, London, 1974.
32 STEENBOCK, F., *Die kirchliche Practeinbände in frühen Mittelalter*, Berlin, 1965.
33 THOMAS, SIR H., *Early Spanish bookbindings, XI–XV centuries*, London, 1939.
34 WEALE, W.H.J., *Bookbindings and rubbings of bindings in the National Art Library, South Kensington*, 2 vols, London, 1894–98.
35 WEISWEILER, M., *Der islamische Bucheinband des Mittelalters*, Wiesbaden, 1962.

B Collections of bindings with reproductions, catalogue and descriptive text

36 DUVAL, K.D., *British bookbinding today* (bookseller's catalogue of a collection of 39 commissioned bindings), Pitlochry, Perthshire, 1975.
37 FLETCHER, W.Y., *English bookbindings in the British Museum*, London, 1895.
38 FLETCHER, W.Y., *Foreign bookbindings in the British Museum*, London, 1896.
39 FOOT, M.M., *The Henry Davis Gift (to the British Library). A collection of bookbindings*, Vol. 1: *Studies in the history of bookbinding*, London, 1978.

40 GELDNER, F., *Bucheinbände aus elf Jahrhunderten. Ausgewählte und beschreiben von F. Geldner* (bindings in the Bavarian State Library), Munich, 1958.
41 GOLDSCHMIDT, E.P., *Gothic and Renaissance bookbindings, exemplified and illustrated from the author's collection*, 2 vols, London, 1928; reprint, Niewkoop, 1967.
42 HARTHAN, J.P., 'Armorial bookbindings from the Clements Collection in the Library of the Victoria and Albert Museum', in *Apollo*, LXXII–LXXV, 1960–61, pp. 179, 186, 165.
43 HOBSON, A.R.A., *French and Italian collectors and their bindings. Illustrated examples from the Library of J.R. Abbey* (Roxburghe Club), Oxford, 1953.
44 HOBSON, G.D., *Bindings in Cambridge libraries*, Cambridge, 1929.
45 HOBSON, G.D., *English bindings 1490–1940 in the Library of J.R. Abbey*, London, 1940.
46 HUESCO ROLLAND, F., *Exposición de encuadernaciones españoles siglos XII al XIX*, Madrid, 1934.
47 HUSUNG, M.J., *Bucheinbände aus der Preussischen Staatsbibliothek zu Berlin*, Leipzig, 1925.
48 LONDON, Victoria and Albert Museum, *Modern British bookbindings by members of Designer Bookbinders* (Exhibition Catalogue), London, 1971.
49 MAZAL, O., *Europaische Einbandkunst aus Mittelalter und Neuzeit; 270 Einbande der Osterreisichchen Nationalbibliothek*, Graz, 1970.
50 MINER, D.E., *The history of bookbinding, 525–1950 A.D.* (Exhibition catalogue, the Walters Art Gallery, Baltimore Museum of Art), Baltimore, Maryland, 1957.
51 NEEDHAM, P., *Twelve centuries of bookbindings: 400–1600* (Exhibition

catalogue, Pierpont Morgan Library, New York, New York, 1979.

52 NIXON, H.M., *Twelve books in fine bindings from the Library of J.W. Hely-Hutchinson* (Roxburghe Club), London, 1953.

53 NIXON, H.M., *Broxbourne Library: styles and designs of bookbindings from the twelfth to the twentieth century (from the collection of Albert Ehrman)*, London, 1956.

54 NIXON, H.M., *Bookbindings from the Library of Jean Grolier* (Exhibition catalogue, British Museum Library, London, 1965.

55 NIXON, H.M., *Sixteenth-century gold-tooled bookbindings in the Pierpont Morgan Library* (Exhibition catalogue), New York, 1971.

56 NIXON, H.M., *English Restoration bookbindings: Samuel Mearne and his contemporaries* (Exhibition catalogue, British Library), London 1974.

57 OLDHAM, J.B., *Shrewsbury School Library bindings*, Oxford, 1943.

58 OXFORD: Bodleian Library, *Fine bindings 1500–1700 from Oxford libraries* (Exhibition catalogue), Oxford, 1968.

59 SCHMIDT, A., *Bucheinbände aus dem XIV.–XIX. Jahrhundertn in der Landesbibliothek zu Darmstadt*, Leipzig, 1921.

C Periodicals

Reports of recent research into specific aspects of bookbinding history are often first published in periodicals, a selection of which is given below.

60 *Archiv für Buchbinderei*, Halle, 1902.

61 *Jahrbuch der Eindbandkust*, 4 vols, Leipzig, 1927–37.

62 *Library (The)*, Series 1–3, London, 1889–1919; Series 4 (Transactions of the Bibliographical Society), 1920–45; Series 5, 1946– .

63 *Transactions of the Cambridge Bibliographical Society*, Cambridge, 1951– .

64 *The Book Collector*, London, 1952–.

65 *Designer Bookbinders' Review*, London, 1973– .

List of illustrations

Note: Bindings listed in W.H.J. Weale's *Catalogue of bookbindings in the National Art Library, South Kensington (1894)* are indicated by their appropriate reference numbers.

1 COPTIC BINDING (fragment): Egypt, ninth century. Blind-tooled goatskin cover, originally stretched on papyrus paste-board, showing leather loop for closing the book. 305 × 235 mm. L.1160–1941.

2 EGYPTIAN: fifteenth century. Brown leather; blind and gold tooling. Cover of a Koran. In the border in Kufic script are some of the Ninety-nine Beautiful Names, or attributes, of Allah. 305 × 235 mm. A.M.1070–1869.

3 EGYPTIAN: fifteenth century. Brown leather; blind and gold tooling. Inner cover of No. 2.

4 PERSIAN: early seventeenth century. Inner cover of red leather; cut leather work on red, blue and green grounds, painted decoration in the inner border on a gold ground. 397 × 260 mm. A.M.452–1888.

5 PERSIAN: *c.* 1680. Red leather; panels stamped in gold, painted relief figures of animals and birds. Bound and signed by Muhammad Muhsin of Tabriz. 235 × 140 mm. L.364–1885. *Nizami, Gangavi: Khusraw wa Shirin* (manuscript written AD1680).

6 PERSIAN: sixteenth century. Lacquered paste-board cover painted in gold and polychrome. 300 × 112 mm. L.353–1885.

7 PERSIAN: seventeenth century, style of Herat. Book cover of crimson leather painted in gold; sunk panels with cut work in white over a black ground. 241 × 133 mm. L.1567–1920.

8 CAROLINGIAN (Palace School, possibly Aachen or Trier): ninth century. Ivory relief after an earlier (sixth-century) East Christian model, probably forming, with a companion ivory now in the Vatican Library, Rome, the covers of a Gospel book from Lorsch Abbey. One part of the manuscript is now at Rome, the other at Karlsburg (formerly in Hungary, now Alba-Iulia, Romania). 375 × 270 mm. A.M.138–1866.

9 GERMAN (Rhenish): tenth or early eleventh century. Beechwood; overlaid with gold, enriched with

cloisonné enamels and semi-
precious stones. The embossed
figure of Christ enthroned and
surrounding foliage date from the
late twelfth century. Upper and
part of the lower inscription res-
tored. Formerly belonging to the
church of Nôtre Dame de Valère,
and subsequently to the cathedral
at Sion, Valais, Switzerland.
254 × 220 mm. A.M.567–1893.
Manuscript *Evangelium*, German,
tenth or early eleventh century.

10 GERMAN: fifteenth century (second
or third quarter). Dark brown calf
over wooden boards decorated in
the *cuir ciselé* technique.
295 × 205 mm. L.1810–1955.
Two manuscript theological tracts
in German, written on paper.

11 GERMAN: *c.* 1470. Brown leather;
blind stamping and tooling with
gilded centres to the large cinquefoils. From the bindery of
Ulrich Schreier, Salzburg.
420 × 285 mm. L.1810–1889.
Durandus, G, *Rationale divinorum
officiorum*, Strassburg, *c.* 1467.

12 GERMAN: *c.* 1472. Brown calf; blind
stamping with the name 'conradus
de argenthina' (i.e., Strassburg),
perhaps the binder, on the outer
border. (Weale 169).
305 × 215 mm. A.L.22 March
1872.
Eybe, A. von, *Margarita poetica*,
Nuremberg, 1472.

13 GERMAN: late fifteenth century.
Brown leather; blind stamping
with metal mounts.
326 × 225 mm. A.L.1904–1883.
Bartholomeus Anglicus, *De prop-
rietatibus rerum*, Nuremberg, 1483.

14 FRENCH: *c.* 1525. Brown calf; blind
tooling with roll-produced borders and vertical strips in centre
panel. 377 × 250 mm. A.L.1492–
1893.

Charlier de Gerson, J., *Quarta pars
operum Joannis de Gerson*, Paris,
1521.

15 SPANISH: *c.* 1470–80. Goatskin over
wooden boards; blind tooling. Five
ornamental brass bosses on upper
cover, the centre boss probably
used for fastening the ties or clasps
fixed to the bottom cover. A *mudéjar* binding made by Moorish
craftsmen. 420 × 290 mm. L.2463–
1950.
Egidio Colonna, *Libro . . . que trata
del regimiento de los principes* (manuscript on paper written. *c.* 1470–80).

16 NETHERLANDISH: *c.* 1540. Brown
calf; blind-tooled panel stamps, in
the centre St Margaret riding
triumphant on a dragon and flanked
by a wyvern and a griffin. (Weale
93). 140 × 82 mm. A.L.1699–1888.
Rosario de la gloriosa Vergina Maria,
Venice, 1536.

17 ENGLISH (?): *c.* 1526. Light brown
calf; blind-tooled panel stamp of St
Roche showing his plague spot.
This stamp was used in the bindery
of John Siberich, a German printer
who settled in Cambridge in 1520,
though the border is not among
those known to have been used by
him. 116 × 113 mm. L.2757–1930.
Rupertus, Abbot of St Heribert at
Deutz, *De divinis officiis libri xii*,
Cologne, 1526.

18 GERMAN: *c.* 1500. Antiphoner
cover. Buckskin; blind tooling,
with embroidered figure of Christ
Crucified, metal mounts and the
original title written on a slip of
vellum. 635 × 425 mm. A.L.17 July
1885.

19 FLEMISH: *c.* 1540. Flemish woodcut
wrapper binding with portrait of
the Emperor Charles V on horseback. 390 × 220 mm. L.3012–1952.
Manuscript rent book, with entries
in French by Michel de la Houe of

properties in or near Mons belonging to his father-in-law, Jehan de la Croix, covering the years 1552–66.

20 ITALIAN: late fifteenth century. Brown calf over wooden boards; blind-tooled cable-work ornament with gilt roundels.
213 × 132 mm. L.937–1951.
Cicero, *De amicitia* (manuscript on vellum, written *c.* 1460).

21 ITALIAN: early sixteenth century. Brown calf; gold tooling.
224 × 150 mm. L.1772–1921.
Bequeathed by David Currie. Book of Hours, written for a member of the Serristori family of Florence (manuscript on vellum written *c,* 1500).

22 ITALIAN: *c.* 1535. Brown calf; gold tooling with painted bands in black, red and white. (Weale 236)
158 × 102 mm. A.M.549–1864.
Caviceo, J., *Il Peregrino*, Venice, 1531.

23 GERMAN: *c.* 1540. Red morocco; gold and blind tooling in the Italian style. Bound at the Fugger bindery, Augsburg, in the Greek fashion with raised headcaps, the boards flush with the leaves and a groove round the three edges of the covers. The Greek technique of forwarding was used in the West for Greek books only. 212 × 147 mm.
A.M.30–1865. Ἐπιστολαὶ διαφόρων φιλοσόφων. *Venice,* 1499.

24 ITALIAN: *c.* 1540. Red morocco; gold tooling, Cameo stamp with Apollo in his chariot and Pegasus on Mount Helicon. Bound for Giovanni Battista Grimaldi (*c.* 1524–*c.* 1612). (Weale 238).
158 × 105 mm. A.M.93–1866.
Malipiero, G., *Il Petrarcha spirituale*, Venice, 1538.

25 ITALIAN (Venetian): 1550. Red leather with sunk panels gilt and painted, perhaps made by oriental craftsmen. The centre medallion contains the Lion of St Mark in painted relief. 227 × 155 mm.
A.M.25–1881.
Manuscript collection of the decrees of the 'Council of Ten', Venice, 1550.

26 FRENCH: *c.* 1531. Black calf; gold tooling. The panel stamp designed by Geofroy Tory (d.1533) and incorporating his personal mark of a cracked vase pierced by a drill or 'toret' in allusion to his name.
191 × 127 mm. L.1402–1931.
Horae in laudem beatiss. Virginis Mariae ad usum Romanum, Paris, 1531.

27 FRENCH: *c.* 1550. Brown morocco; gold tooling. By the 'Pecking Crow' binder. (Weale 245).
158 × 100 mm. A.M.32–1865.
Suetonius, *Le vite de dodici Cesari tradotte in lingua Toscano per M.P. de Rosso*, Venice, 1550.

28 FRENCH: *c.* 1550.. Brown calf; gold tooling with black painted decoration incorporating the arms of Thomas Wotton (1521–1587). The armorial stamp of four quarterings in the centre is impressed in silver and black, an early example of an attempt to reproduce the correct heraldic tinctures. Bequeathed by Henry J.B. Clements, Esq.
290 × 197 mm. L.1593–1948.
Koran, Basle, 1543.

29 FRENCH: *c.* 1550. Brown calf; gold tooling, with traces of the painted arms of Edward VI of England. Probably by one of Thomas Wotton's binders. 345 × 240 mm.
L.530–1937.
New Testament in Greek, Paris, 1550.

30 FRENCH: *c.* 1560. Light-brown calf; gold tooling. From the *atelier au trèfle* of Claude de Piques, with two

examples of the trefoil tool, much used by this bindery, in the centre. 210 × 134 mm. L.709–1939.
Bocchi, A., *Symbolicorum quaestionum de universo genere quas serio ludebat libri cinque*, Bologna, 1555.

31 FRENCH: *c.* 1555. Light brown calf and morocco; gold tooling with black and white painted strapwork. Bound in the Lyonese style. The panels on the covers and spine appear to be calf, the edges of the covers and the joints in moroco leather. 128 × 70 mm. A.M.7925–1862.
Dante, *Commediae divina con nuove et utili ispositioni*, Lyons, 1551.

32 GERMAN: *c.* 1572. Pigskin; blind stamping and tooling, with four panels in the centre bearing the signature or initials of the Wittenberg binder Thomas Krüger, and representing Charles V, Johann Friedrich I, Duke of Saxony, Luther and Melanchthon. Roll-produced bands of religious and allegorical subjects at top and bottom. (Weale 192). 326 × 210 mm. A.L.1186–1885.
Cureus, J., *Gentis Silesiae annales*, Wittenberg 1571.

33 SPANISH: *c.* 1595. Brown calf; gold tooling, roll-produced borders and small individual tools. A Granada binding. 328 × 216 mm. L.116–1938.
Illuminated manuscript attestation of nobility granted to Martín Lopez Cana of Jérez de la Frontera. Dated Granada, 29 May 1595.

34 ENGLISH: *c.* 1600. Brown calf; gold tooling. Centre-piece of foliated strap- and scroll-work on a stippled ground enclosing a crowned falcon. This was a badge used by Elizabeth I, but its appearance on a binding does not necessarily indicate royal ownership; the royal arms and

badges occur frequently on 'trade' bindings. (Weale 9).
283 × 192 mm. Dyce Collection 9154.
Bequeathed by the Rev. Alexander Dyce. Sidney, Sir Philip, *The Countesse of Pembroke's Arcadia*, London, 1598.

35 ENGLISH: *c.* 1590. Brown calf; gold tooling, with armorial stamp of twenty-one quarterings of Gilbert Talbot (1552–1616), 7th Earl of Shrewsbury. 220 × 165 mm. L.2177–1948.
Bequeathed by Henry J.B. Clements, Esq.
Yonge, N., *Musica transalpina* (tenor part only of a book of madrigals).

36 FRENCH: *c.* 1580. Brown morocco; gold tooling with the strapwork painted in black and the volute tool in grey. Centre medallion of the Crucifixion. An early fanfare binding. 195 × 125 mm. A.M.31–1865.
Missale Romanum, Antwerp, 1577.

37 FRENCH: *c.* 1595. Red morocco; gold tooling. 'Marguerite' – style binding with the arms of Pietro Duodo, Venetian Ambassador to France 1594–97, in the centre oval. 125 × 80 mm. L.3856–1979.
Elder, D.G., *Methodus catechismi Catholici*, Lyons, 1579; Junilus, E.A., *De partibus divinae legis*, Paris, 1556 (2 vols bound in one).

38 FRENCH: *c.* 1640. Brown morocco; gold tooling. Arms of Louis XIII (1610–43) surrounded by the collars of the Orders of St Michael and St Esprit, enclosed in a wreath of oak leaves, on a semis of fleurs-de-lys and crowned L's. Probably a 'trade' binding. (Weale 153.)
236 × 175 mm. A.L.1887–1884.
Polybii, Diodori Siculi et aliorum excerpta ex collectaneis C.A. Porphyrogenetae, Paris, 1634.

39 FRENCH: *c.* 1640. Red morocco; fanfare design with gold pointillé tooling. Probably bound by Florimond Badier, unsigned but with his personal emblem of a profile head in the four corners. 180 × 122 mm. L.795–1938. *Ἀνακρεντος Τηϊου τα μελη. Paris,* 1639.

40 ENGLISH: *c.* 1640. Brown morocco; gold tooling. Bound at Little Gidding, Huntingdonshire, perhaps by Mary Ferrar. 190 × 140 mm. L.538–1937. Valdes, J. de, *The Hundred and Ten Considerations,* Oxford, 1638.

41 ENGLISH: 1613. Embroidered book cover worked by Elizabeth Illingworth and dated 1613. Silk on linen canvas, mainly tent stitch. The covers depict Old Testament scenes: Abraham about to sacrifice Isaac and Jonah being cast up by the whale. 228 × 160 mm. T.134–1929. Holy Bible, Geneva, 1610.

42a ENGLISH: *c.* 1655. Vellum; gold tooling with appliqués of red, black and citron turkey. Fore-edge painting under gold of flowers and a wreath with the words 'Search the Scriptures John 5. 39', and the signature below 'Lewis *fecit*'. 175 × 120 mm. L.794–1938. Holy Bible, London, 1651 (colophon 1655).

42b Signed fore-edge painting of No. 42 'Search the Scriptures John 5. 39'.

43 ENGLISH: *c.* 1685. Dark red turkey; gold tooling with the interlacing fillet and some of the ornaments stained black. Signed 'Cleeve' (upper cover) '*Fecit*' (lower cover). An English fanfare binding. 195 × 125 mm. L.1849–1939. Book of Common Prayer, London, 1680.

44 ENGLISH: *c.* 1690. Black turkey; gold tooling with red and citron onlays. A 'cottage'-style binding. (Weale 48). 155 × 85 mm. A.L.1408–1886. Book of Common Prayer, London, 1686.

45 ENGLISH: *c.* 1689–90. Dark red turkey; gold tooling. In the 'cottage' style, possibly from the bindery of Robert Steel. 865 × 560 mm. L.1525–1939. Presented by Lady Marjorie Pentland; formerly owned by her mother Isabel, Marchioness of Aberdeen, and by her grandfather, the first Lord Tweedmouth who 'collected bindings and used them as albums' according to his granddaughter. Covers relaid on an album of blank leaves.

46 ENGLISH: *c.* 1670. Dark brown turkey; gold and blind tooling, with silvered bands, 'drawer-handle' ornaments and fleurons. 372 × 241 mm. L.1414–1904. Book of Common Prayer, London, 1662.

47 ENGLISH: early eighteenth century. Black turkey; gold tooling. From the bindery of Elkanah Settle. Arms of Compton, possibly Spencer Compton, MP, Speaker of the House of Commons. 295 × 185 mm. L.607–1938. Presented by Lieutenant-Colonel W.E. Moss. Settle, E., *Carmen irenicum. The union of the imperial crowns of England,* London, 1707.

48 ITALIAN: *c.* 1662. Black morocco; gold tooling. Roll-produced border. Fan pattern. (Weale 271) 238 × 165 mm. 17.vi.1878. *Andriae Mariani lessus,* Bologna, 1662.

49 GERMAN: *c.* 1710–20. Light brown calf; gold tooling. In the centre the arms of Ettal Abbey, Bavaria.

332 × 210 mm. A.L.1591–1885. Covers relaid on an album of blank leaves.

50 SCOTTISH: *c.* 1750. Brown morocco; gold tooling. 240 × 180 mm. L.1275–1889.
Ewart, R., *Dissertatio medica inauguralis de scrofula*, Edinburgh, 1749.

51 IRISH: 1779. Red morocco, inlaid white paper centre-piece; gold tooling, roll-produced border. (Weale 87) 160 × 96 mm. A.L.314–1888. *The Gentleman's and Citizen's Almanack*, Dublin, 1779.

52 ENGLISH: *c.* 1770. Mottled brown calf; gold tooled with a chinoiserie design by Johann Ernst Baumgarten. 220 × 140 mm. A.M.163–1864.
Montague, E., *An Essay on the Writings and Genius of Shakespeare*, London, 1770.

53 ENGLISH: *c.* 1776. Red morocco; gold tooling. Chinoiserie binding with the armorial stamp of Philip Stanhope (1755–1815), 5th Earl of Chesterfield, 418 × 177 mm. L.1857–1948.
Bequeathed by Henry J.B. Clements, Esq.
Book of Common Prayer, Oxford, 1766.

54 ENGLISH: *c.* 1795. Pink, green and yellow stained calf, with a centre ornament engraved in black and varnished. Gold-tooled outer borders and fillets. 230 × 145 mm. L.708–1939.
Bate, J., *A Rationale of the Literal Doctrine of Original Sin*, London, 1766.

55 ENGLISH: *c.* 1800. Brown calf stained to imitate the terracotta shades of Greek and Etruscan pottery; gold-tooled borders with black painted classical ornament. 222 × 138 mm. L.951–1948.
Bequeathed by Henry J.B. Clements, Esq.

Bryan, M., *A Compendious System of Astronomy*, 2nd ed., London, 1799.

56 ENGLISH: *c.* 1785. Scenery binding by Edwards of Halifax. Vellum; gold tooling, with an undercover painting of Westgate Street, Wakefield, Yorkshire, in the style of James Malton or Edward Dayes, perhaps copied from a print. The large house on the right is Milnes House, built by John Milnes (d. 1771) in 1750 and demolished in 1854–66 when Westgate Station was built. On the spine is a wheatsheaf crest and the initials JM belonging to another member of the Milnes family. 216 × 290 mm. L.1601–1953.
The Virtuosi's Museum: containing selected Views in England, Scotland and Ireland drawn by Paul Sandby, London, 1788.

57 ENGLISH: *c.* 1790. Gold-tooled borders with a painting, under transparent vellum of an allegorical figure representing Fame. Lower cover of No. 56. L.1601–1953.

58a ENGLISH: *c.* 1790. Green morocco; gold tooling. Bound by Roger Payne. 168 × 105 mm. L.1791–1934.
Caesar, *Opera*, Venice, 1519.

58b ENGLISH: *c.* 1790. Green morocco; gold tooling, with a centre panel of paper. Doublure of No. 58a.

59 ENGLISH: *c.* 1770–80. Red morocco; gold tooling. Armorial stamp of the Rev. Mordaunt Cracherode designed and cut by Roger Payne. 233 × 123 mm. L. 2324–1948.
Bequeathed by Henry J.B. Clements Esq.
Alcyonius, P., *De exsilio*. Venice, 1522.

60 ENGLISH: *c.* 1791. Citron morocco, inlaid with black and morocco and gold tooled to a repeating pattern.

Bound by L. Staggemeier and Samuel Welcher. 249 × 167 mm. L.3061–1967.
Walpole, Horace, The Castle of Otranto. Parma, 1791.

61 ENGLISH: c. 1805. Crimson cross-grained morocco; gold tooling with an initial C beneath a royal crown for Queen Charlotte (d.1818), wife of George III. Bound by Charles Meyer, a German immigrant, with his label on fly-leaf: 'Bookseller & Binder to the Queen & Princesses'. 215 × 280 mm. L.5462–1976. *Description of Latium; or, La Campagna di Roma, London, 1805.*

62 FRENCH: c. 1775. Crimson morocco; gold tooled dentelle border with small bird tool frequently found on Derome-le-Jeune bindings. 350 × 250 mm. L.1533–1949. *Sallust, La conjuracion de Catilina y la guerra de Jugurta, Madrid, 1772.*

63 FRENCH: 1786. Red morocco; broad dentelle border with scrolls, scallops and lattice-work, stamped from a metal plate by Dubuisson in use in 1754. 245 × 175 mm. A.M.995–1897. *Almanach Royal, Paris, 1786.*

64 FRENCH: c. 1814. Red morocco; gold and blind tooling with roll-produced border. Restoration binding attributed to Comte Auguste de Caumont, a French emigré who established a bindery in London during the Revolution. 296 × 225 mm. A.L.2040–1883. *Lille, J. de, Le malheur et la pitié, London, 1814.*

65 ENGLISH: c. 1820. Red morocco; gold and blind tooling with a design in the 'cathedral' style. 203 × 148 mm. A.L.1674–1902. Bequeathed by George Reid, Esq. Manuscript Book of Hours (Flemish), second half of fifteenth century (Reid MS. 30).

66 FRENCH: c. 1830 (?). Dark blue morocco; gold and blind tooling. Crowned cypher of King Louis-Philippe (reigned 1830–48) in the centre, with Napoleonic eagles in the inner panel and the initial N under the imperial crown in the four corners. Signed 'Simier, R. du Roi' at foot of upper cover with his label inside 'Simier. Relieur de Roi . . . Medaille d'argent, &c. 1827'. 675 × 495 mm. A.L.558–1881. *Napoleon à la Grande Armée: à la Calcographie du Musée Napoleon, Paris, 1810.*

67 BELGIAN or FRENCH: c. 1836. Dark blue morocco; covers stamped in blind, the spine tooled in gold. 210 × 135 mm. L.3595–1951. *Du Mont de Florgy, Baron A., Les antiquités de Rome, Brussels, 1836.*

68 SPANISH: 1862. Crimson morocco; gold tooling with a centre stamp of the Spanish royal arms, in the 'Second Rococo', mid-nineteenth-century style. 173 × 110 mm. L.3564–1972. *Guia de Forasteros en Madrid para el año de 1862, Madrid, 1861.*

69 FRENCH: c. 1895. Green morocco, with red and blue onlays; gold tooling. The design incorporates objects associated with the dance. Bound by Salvator David. 290 × 195 mm. L.2211–1953. *Legrand, L., Cours de danse fin de siècle, Paris, 1892.*

70 FRENCH: c. 1901. Black morocco, with blue, green and citron onlays; gold tooling; inlaid and incised brown and green leather, the design showing the influence of the Marius-Michel bindery. Bound by Georges Canape. 325 × 258 mm. A.M.950–1901. *Bedier, J., Le roman de Tristan et Iseult, Paris, 1900.*

71 ENGLISH: c. 1900. Brown morocco,

with blue, green and citron onlays; gold tooling. Designed and signed by the Guild of Women Binders, Hampstead. 195 × 125 mm. L.1769–1958.
Marcus Aurelius by himself; an English translation by G.H. Rendell, London, 1901.

72 ENGLISH: *c.* 1899. Buff morocco; embossed design with brass studs, the title tooled in gold. The lower cover is undecorated except for a small trefoil ornament containing the initials MGH – i.e., Mary G. Houston who designed the binding. 202 × 125 mm. L.1969–1899. Omar Khayyam, *Rubaiyat, rendered into English verse (by E. Fitzgerald),* London, 1898.

73 ENGLISH: *c.* 1895. Light brown calf, embossed and incised; gold tooling. Designed by Alice Shepherd and Miss A.M. Bassett, bound by Arthur Smallbone and W. Fazakerley. Signed inside upper cover 'Fazakerley Binder Liverpool'. 327 × 258 mm. L.323–1898. Cover of a blank-leaved album.

74 ENGLISH: 1904. Blue morocco; gold tooling. Designed by Cobden-Sanderson and bound at the Doves Press bindery. 345 × 216 mm. L.1583–1922.
Landor, W.S., *Pericles and Aspasia,* New York, 1903.

75 ENGLISH: *c.* 1911. Brown cape goat (morocco?); gold tooling. Bound by Captain Charles Elsden Gladstone, RN (d.1919). 254 × 190 mm. L.1991–1923. Presented by his widow Mrs J.B. Wickham.
Swinburne, A.C., *Songs before Sunrise,* London, 1909.

76 ENGLISH: 1927. Green morocco; gold tooling with red centres to the small circular tools. Designed by Douglas Cockerell and bound in the Douglas Cockerell and Son bindery. 295 × 192 mm. L.1141–1938.
Apuleius, *De Cupidinis et Psyches amoribus,* London, 1901.

77 ENGLISH: 1928. Red morocco; gold tooling with inlaid green frame around the centre panel. Designed and bound by William Matthews. 189 × 122 mm. L.1315–1962. Victoria and Albert Museum, *A Picture Book of Book-Bindings,* London, 1927.

78 ENGLISH: *c.* 1923. Buff morocco; inlaid with light brown leather; gold tooling. Designed and bound by Madeleine Kohn. 222 × 166 mm. L.1048–1931. Jammes, F., *Pomme d'anis,* Paris, 1923.

79 ENGLISH: 1934. Black morocco, with orange inlays; gold tooling. Designed and bound by Sybil Pye. 313 × 202 mm. L.494–1938. Presented by Miss Sybil Pye. The Bible: *The Apocrypha, reprinted according to the Authorised Version, 1611,* London 1924.

80 ENGLISH: *c.* 1926. Purple morocco; gold and blind tooling. Designed by Robert Ashwin Maynard and bound by George Fisher at the Gregynog Press bindery, Montgomeryshire, Wales. 268 × 178 mm. L.2497–1938. Thomas, E., *Chosen Essays,* London, 1926.

81 ENGLISH: *c.* 1930. Red morocco; gold tooling. Designed by Charles Ricketts. 257 × 190 mm. L.1818–1958. Raymond, J.P., *Beyond the Threshold. Translated from the French and illustrated by Charles Rickeetts,* privately printed, 1929.

82 FRENCH: 1950. Dark blue morocco, with fawn onlays; gold and blind tooling. Designed by Pierre Legrain

and bound by Jacques Anthoine–Legrain. 298 × 228 mm. L.800–1951.
Nodier, C., *Histoire du chien de Brisquet*, Paris, 1900.

83 FRENCH: 1951. Grey morocco, with perforated mosaic inlay over coloured leathers; gold and blind tooling. Designed and bound by Rose Adler. 450 × 334 mm. L.1574–1945.
Rouault, G., *Cirque de l'étoile filante*, Paris, 1938.

84 FRENCH: 1949. Fawn morocco, with dark brown raised calf onlays. Designed by Henri Creuzevault. 367 × 277 mm. L.1187–1946.
Picasso, *Eaux-fortes originales pour des textes de Buffon*, Paris, 1942.

85 FRENCH: 1963. Black, grey and white morocco with onlays of similar colours; the title, together with the names of the author and illustrator, appear alternately or (to borrow an heraldic term) counterchanged in black and grey in the shutter-like design in perspective on the covers. Designed by Pierre-Lucien Martin. 513 × 331 mm. L.3986–1965.
Frenaud, A., *Enorme figure de la déesse raison: poème orné d'une gravure originale par Raoul Ubac* (the source for the cover design), Paris, 1950.

86 ENGLISH: 1957. Natural-toned vellum; gold tooling. Bound by Sydney M. Cockerell with calligraphic decoration by Joan Tebbutt. 193 × 140 mm. L.3189–1958.
Shakespeare. *Complete Works*, Edited, with a Glossary, by W.J. Craig, London, 1954.

87 ENGLISH: 1960. Green oasis morocco; gold and blind tooling. Designed and bound by Roger Powell. 310 × 185 mm. L.3717–1960.

Chaucer, Geoffrey, *Troilus and Cressida*, London, 1939.

88 ENGLISH: 1962. Buff morocco; inlaid design of black and brown onlays with black tooling. Designed and bound by Edgar Mansfield. One of a series of variant bindings designed for this book. 262 × 196 mm. L.2390–1962.
Bates, H.E., *Through the Woods. The English Woodland April to April. With 73 Engravings on Wood by Agnes Miller Parker*, London, 1936.

89 ENGLISH: 1966. Purple and blue morocco; both covers decorated with multicoloured feathered onlays impressed with symbolic figures in gold, the concentric circles on the upper cover representing the castles in *Hamlet, Macbeth* and other plays, surrounded by representational defenders about to be confronted by black swarms of attackers. Designed and bound by Philip Smith. 280 × 218 mm. L.3378–1966.
Shakespeare, *Ten Great Plays: illustrated by Alice and Martin Provensen*, London, 1962.

90 ENGLISH: 1972. Purple oasis; gold tooling with coloured onlays with the 'clouds' motif pioneered by the binder. Designed and bound by Elizabeth Greenhill. 252 × 168 mm. L.3992–1972.
Graves, R., *The Green-Sailed Vessel: Poems*. London, 1971.

91 ENGLISH: 1977. Medium brown oasis goatskin with onlays of beige goatskin, black calf and white calf. Designed and bound by Ivor Robinson. 385 × 290 mm. L.835–1954.
Virgil, *Le Georgiche di Virgilio, (versione italiana di G. Capriri con acquaforti di Manzu)*, Milan, 1948.

LINE ILLUSTRATIONS

The relationship between bookbinders' decorative tools and printers' flowers may be seen in the ornamental borders reproduced on some of the pages of this book, which have been adapted from bindings in the Museum collections.

FRONT COVER: The corner pieces are taken from plate 23 (*German c. 1540*)

TITLE PAGE: The corner pieces are taken from plate 24 (*Italian c. 1540*) and the centre decoration from plate 27 (*French c. 1550*)

CONTENTS PAGE AND PAGE 38: The decorations are taken from illustration 24 (*Italian c. 1540*)

PAGE 7: The decoration is taken from plate 27 (*French c. 1550*)

PAGE 41: The decoration is taken from plate 77 (*English 1928*)

I COPTIC BINDING Egypt, ninth century.
305 × 235 mm.

2 EGYPTIAN: fifteenth century.
305 × 235 mm.

3 EGYPTIAN: fifteenth century.
Inner cover of No. 2.

54

Opposite
4 PERSIAN: end of sixteenth century.
397 × 260 mm.

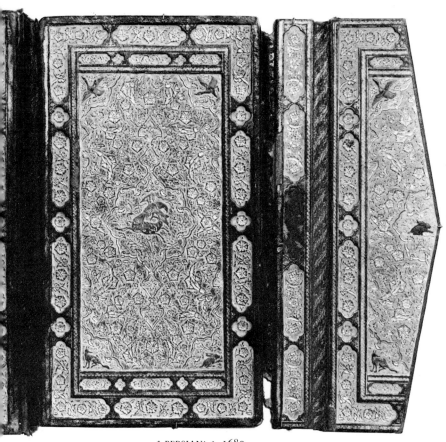

5 PERSIAN: *c.* 1680.
235 × 140 mm.

Opposite
6 PERSIAN: sixteenth century.
300 × 112 MM.

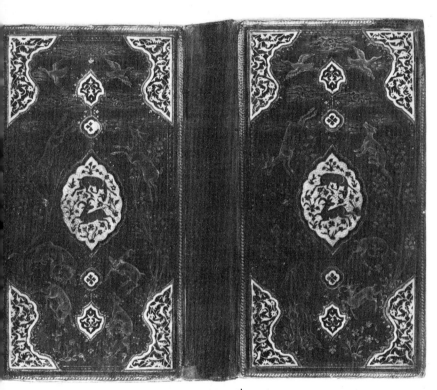

7 PERSIAN: seventeenth century.
241 × 133 mm.

Opposite
8 CAROLINGIAN (Palace School) ninth century.
375 × 270 mm.

9 GERMAN (Rhenish): tenth or early eleventh century.
254 × 220 mm.

10 GERMAN: fifteenth century (second or third quarter).
295 × 205 mm.

11 GERMAN: *c.* 1470.
420 × 285 mm.

12 GERMAN: *c.* 1472.
305 × 215 mm.

13 GERMAN: late fifteenth century.
326 × 225 mm.

14 FRENCH: *c.* 1525.
377 × 250 mm.

15 SPANISH: *c.* 1470–80.
420 × 290 mm.

Below
16 NETHERLANDISH: *c.* 1540.
140 × 82 mm.

Opposite
17 ENGLISH (?): *c.* 1526.
116 × 113 mm.

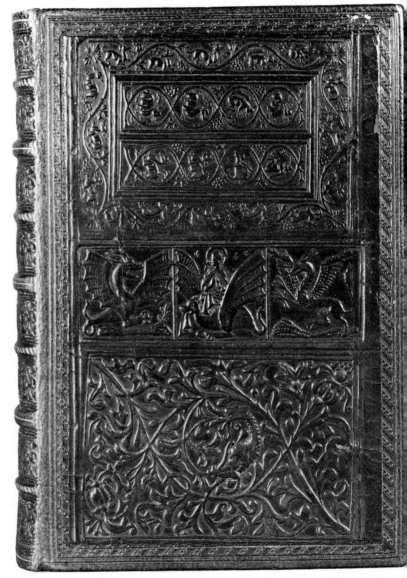

Sancte roche oz.

18 GERMAN: *c.* 1500.
635 × 425 mm.

Opposite
19 FLEMISH: *c.* 1540.
390 × 220 mm.

Opposite
20 ITALIAN: late fifteenth century.
213 × 132 mm.

21 ITALIAN: early sixteenth century.
224 × 150 mm.

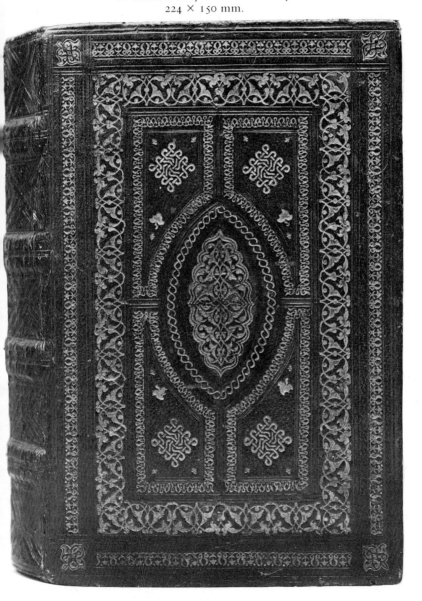

Right
22 ITALIAN: *c.* 1535.
158 × 102 mm.

Below
23 GERMAN: *c.* 1540.
212 × 147 mm.

Opposite
24 ITALIAN: *c.* 1540.
158 × 105 mm.

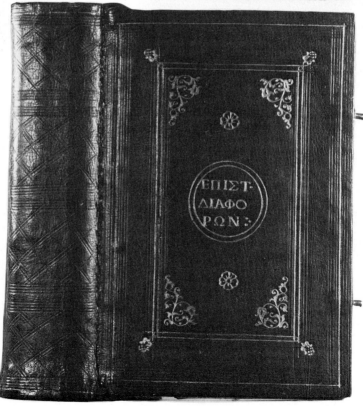

25 ITALIAN (Venetian): 1550.
227 × 155 mm.

Opposite
26 FRENCH: *c.* 1531.
191 × 127 mm.

27 FRENCH: *c.* 1550.
158 × 100 mm.

Opposite
28 FRENCH: *c.* 1550.
290 × 197 mm.

Opposite
29 FRENCH: *c.* 1550.
345 × 240 mm.

30 FRENCH: *c.* 1560.
210 × 134 mm.

31 FRENCH: *c.* 1555.
128 × 70 mm.

Opposite
32 GERMAN: *c.* 1572.
326 × 210 mm.

33 SPANISH: *c.* 1595.
328 × 216 mm.

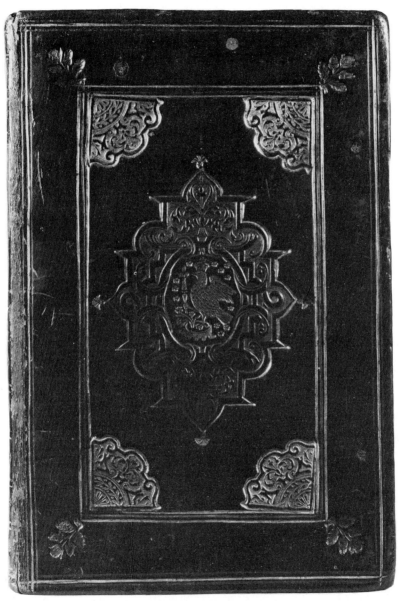

34 ENGLISH: *c.* 1600.
283 × 192 mm.

35 ENGLISH: *c.* 1590.
220 × 165 mm.

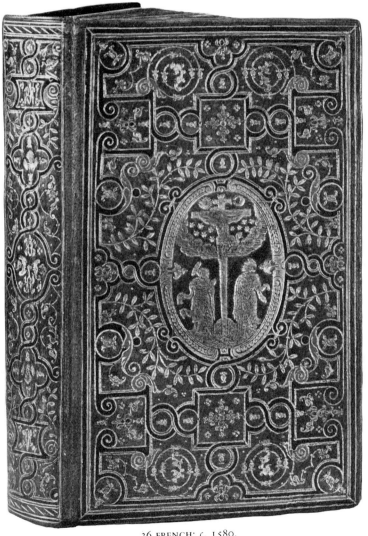

36 FRENCH: *c.* 1580.
195 × 125 mm.

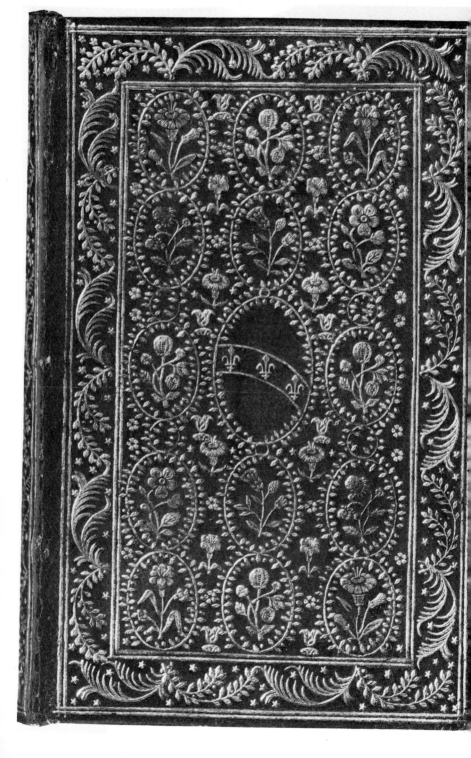

Opposite
37 FRENCH: *c.* 1595.
125 × 80 mm.

38 FRENCH: *c.* 1640.
236 × 175 mm.

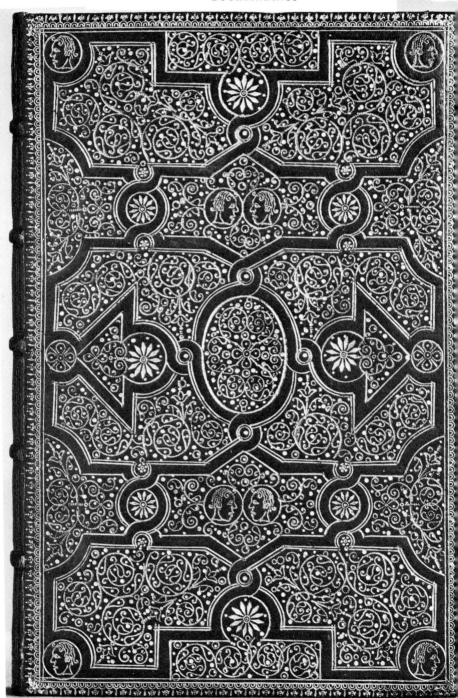

Opposite
39 FRENCH: *c.* 1640.
180 × 122 mm.

40 ENGLISH: *c.* 1640.
190 × 140 mm.

41 ENGLISH: 1613.
228 × 160 mm.

42a ENGLISH:
c. 1655.
175 × 120 mm.

42b Signed fore-
edge painting of
No. 42a.

43 ENGLISH: c. 1685.
195 × 125 mm.

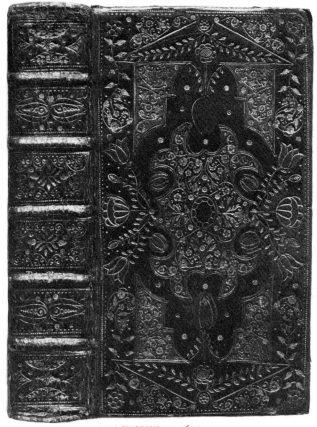

44 ENGLISH: *c.* 1690.
155 × 85 mm.

Opposite
45 ENGLISH: *c.* 1689–90.
865 × 560 mm.

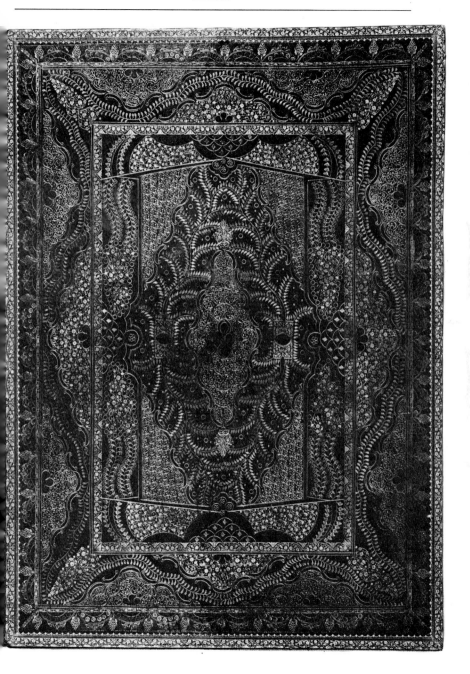

46 ENGLISH: *c.* 1670.
372 × 241 mm.

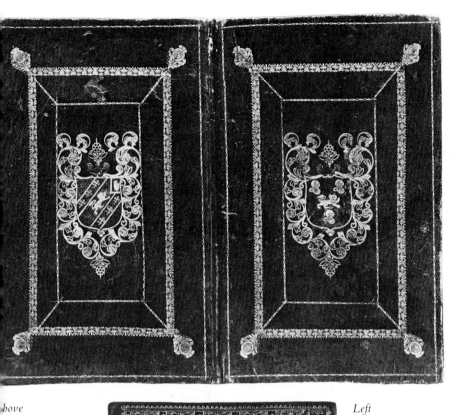

Above
ENGLISH:
Early eighteenth
century.
95 × 185 mm.

Left
48 ITALIAN: *c.* 1662.
238 × 165 mm.

Opposite
49 GERMAN: *c.* 1710–20.
332 × 210 mm.

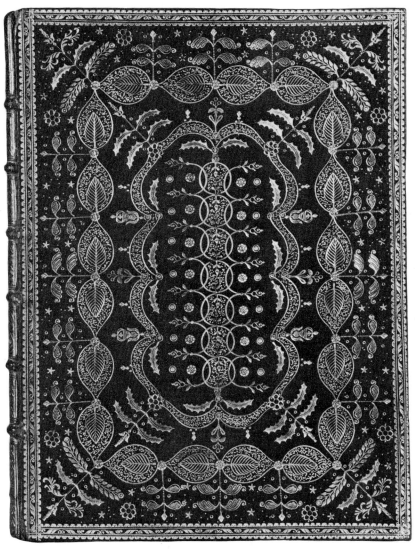

50 SCOTTISH: *c.* 1750.
240 × 180 mm.

51 IRISH: 1779.
160 × 96 mm.

Opposite
52 ENGLISH: *c.* 1770.
220 × 140 mm.

Opposite
53 ENGLISH: *c.* 1776.
418 × 177 mm.

54 ENGLISH: *c.* 1795.
230 × 145 mm.

55 ENGLISH: *c.* 1800.
222 × 138 mm.

Opposite above
56 ENGLISH: *c.* 1785.
216 × 290 mm.

Opposite below
57 ENGLISH: *c.* 1790.
Lower cover of No. 56.

58a ENGLISH: *c.* 1790.
168 × 105 mm.

58b ENGLISH: *c.* 1790.
Doublure of No. 58a.

59 ENGLISH: *c.* 1770–80.
223 × 123 mm.

60 ENGLISH: *c.* 1791.
249 × 167 mm.

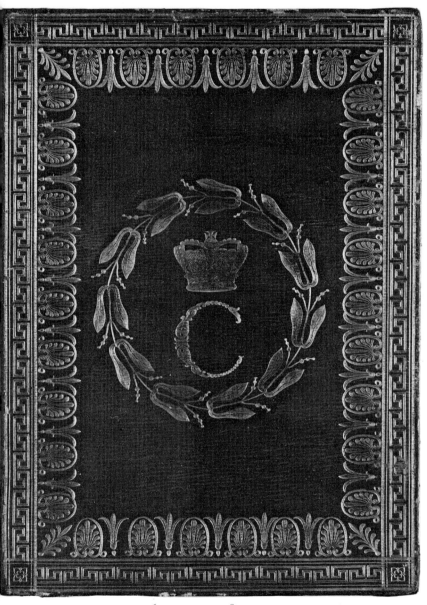

61 ENGLISH: *c.* 1805.
215 × 280 mm.

62 FRENCH: *c.* 1775.
350 × 250 mm.

63 FRENCH: 1786.
245 × 175 mm.

64 FRENCH: *c.* 1814.
296 × 225 mm.

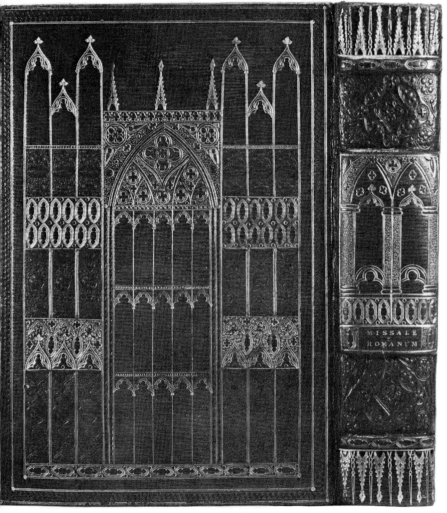

65 ENGLISH: *c.* 1820.
203 × 148 mm.

PLATES

Opposite
66 FRENCH: *c.* 1830 (?).
675 × 495 mm.

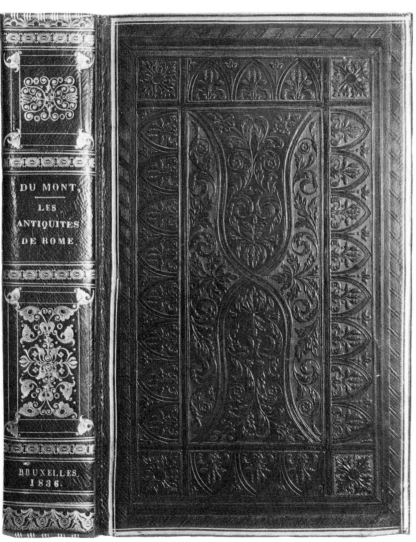

67 BELGIAN or FRENCH: *c.* 1836.
210 × 135 mm.

68 SPANISH: 1862.
173 × 110 mm.

Opposite
69 FRENCH: *c.* 1895.
290 × 195 mm.

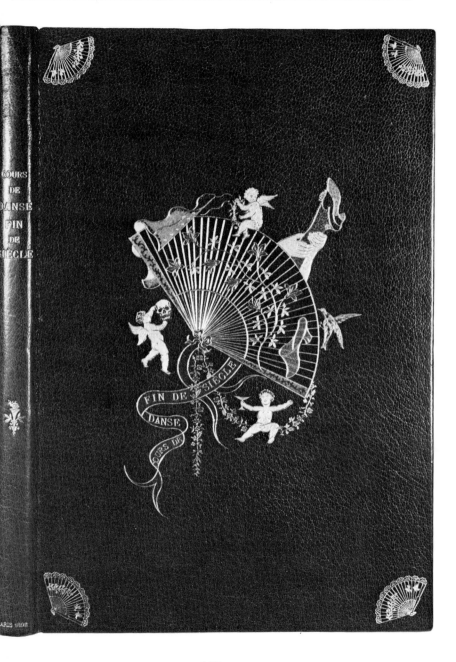

Opposite
70 FRENCH: *c*. 1901.
325 × 258 mm.

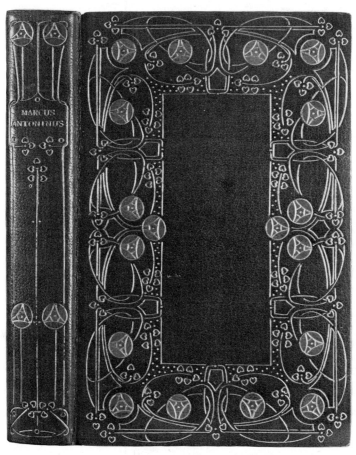

71 ENGLISH: *c*. 1900.
195 × 125 mm.

Opposite
72 ENGLISH: *c.* 1899.
202 × 125 mm.

73 ENGLISH: *c.* 1895.
327 × 258 mm.

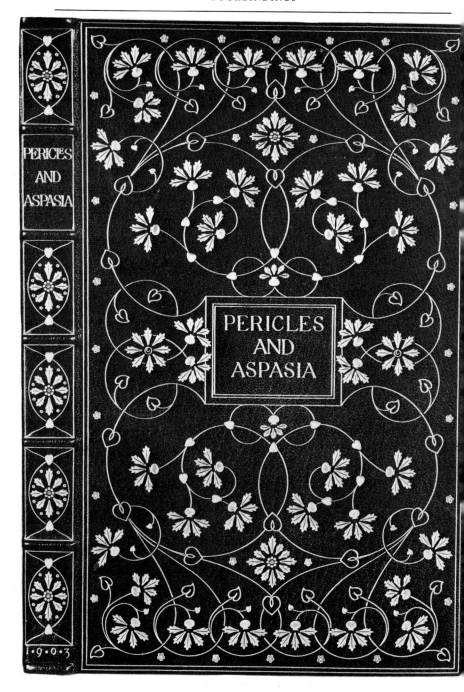

Opposite
74 ENGLISH: 1904.
345 × 216 mm.

75 ENGLISH: *c.* 1911.
254 × 190 mm.

76 ENGLISH: *c.* 1927.
295 × 192 mm.

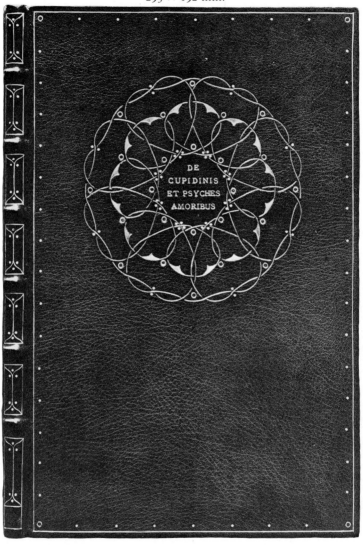

DE
CUPIDINIS
ET PSYCHES
AMORIBUS

Opposite
77 ENGLISH: 1928.
189 × 122 mm.

78 ENGLISH: *c.* 1923.
222 × 166 mm.

Opposite
79 ENGLISH: 1934.
313 × 202 mm.

80 ENGLISH: *c.* 1926.
268 × 178 mm.

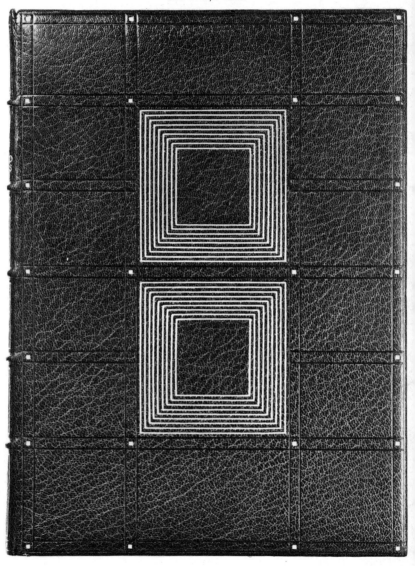

Opposite
81 ENGLISH: *c.* 1930.
257 × 190 mm.

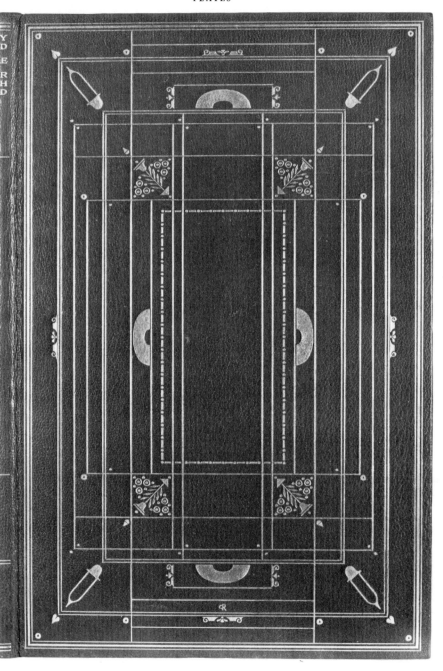

82 FRENCH: 1950.
298 × 228 mm.

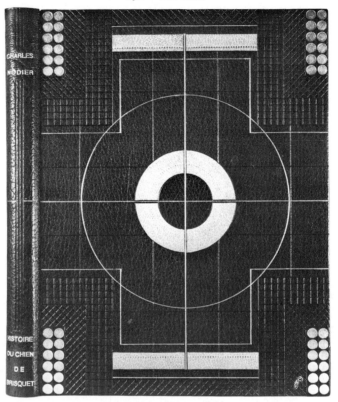

Opposite above
83 FRENCH: 1951.
450 × 334 mm.

Opposite below
84 FRENCH: 1949.
367 × 277 mm.

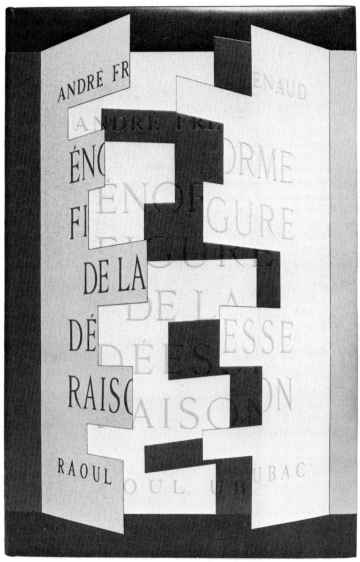

85 FRENCH: 1963.
513 × 331 mm.

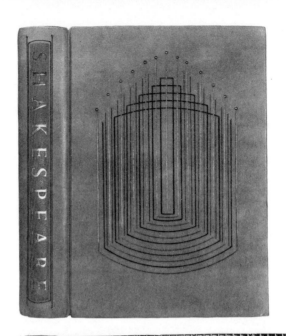

86 ENGLISH: 1957.
193 × 140 mm.

87 ENGLISH: 1960.
310 × 185 mm.

88 ENGLISH: 1962.
262 × 196 mm.

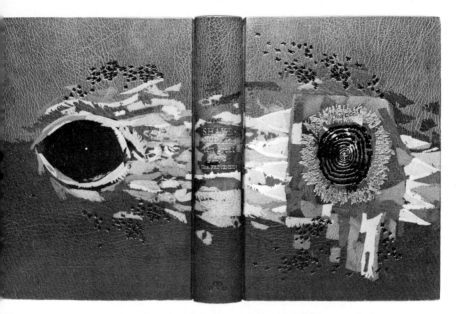

Above
89 ENGLISH: 1966.
280 × 218 mm.

Left
90 ENGLISH: 1972.
252 × 168 mm.

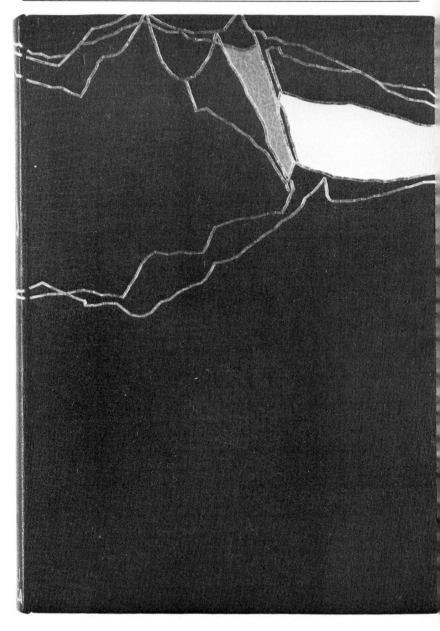

91 ENGLISH: 1977.
385 × 290 mm.

Colour Plates

1 FRENCH: c. 1555–65. Brown calf; gold tooling with black painted strapwork. Bound by Grolier's Last Binder. 393 × 256 mm. L.3395–1938.
Steucho, A., *Enarrationum in Psalmos pars prima*, Lyons, 1548.

2 GERMAN: 1583. Brown calf; gold tooling. Centre medallion with the figure of Religion holding a chalice, surrounded by the initials of Friedrich August Herzog Zu Sachsen (Duke of Saxony, d.1586). Roll-produced borders incorporating the arms of Saxony and Denmark. Bound by Caspar Meuser of Dresden (d.1593). 310 × 192 mm. 9.xii.1867.
Luther, M., *Der erste Teil aller Bücher und Schriften*, Jena, 1575.

3 ITALIAN: c. 1612. Red morocco; gold tooling. Fanfare-type design. 360 × 243 mm. 18.xii.1869.
Pontificale Romanum, Rome, 1611.

4 ENGLISH: c. 1672. Red turkey; gold tooling with coloured onlays and painted strapwork. 370 × 235 mm. A.L.2000–1884.
Newcastle, William Cavendish, Duke of, *Methode nouvelle et invention extraordinaire de dresser les chevaux*, London, 1671.

5 FRENCH: c. 1745–50. White calf; centre-and-corner design with onlays of red, blue, green and citron morocco. Mosaic binding probably designed and bound by Jacques–Antoine Derome l'aîné. In the centre of each cover is the monogram MA beneath a wreath, probably for Mary Arundell (1716–69), wife of the 7th Baron Arundell, or her daughter-in-law Mary Christina Arundell (1743–1813), wife of the 8th Baron, whose ownership label is pasted inside the upper cover. Queen Marie-Antoinette at a later date (c. 1770) used a very similar monogram when Dauphine of France. 199 × 129 mm. L.3737–1964.
Heures présentées à Madame la Dauphine, Paris (c. 1745).

6 GERMAN: c. 1826. Grey morocco; gold tooling with a coloured inlaid centre design of a rose window. Bound in the cathedral style by Johann Jacob Selencka of Brunswick. 315 × 250 mm. L.491–1971.
Planché, J., *Oberon. Romantische Oper in drey Acten. Musik von Carl Maria von Weber. Klavier-Auszug von Componisten*, Berlin, 1826.

7 FRENCH: 1952. Mosaic decoration of various coloured inlaid calf leathers, the colours and design inspired by Matisse's illustrations in the book. Designed by Paul Bonet. 470 × 348 mm. L.338–1948.
Matisse, H., *Jazz*, Paris, 1947.

8 ENGLISH: 1980. Undyed oasis with grey and multi-coloured mosaic recessed onlays; blind and gold tooling. Designed and bound by Sally Lou Smith. 350 × 210 mm. L.2211–1982. Presented by John P. Harthan. Harthan, J.P. *Books of Hours and their Owners*. London, 1977.

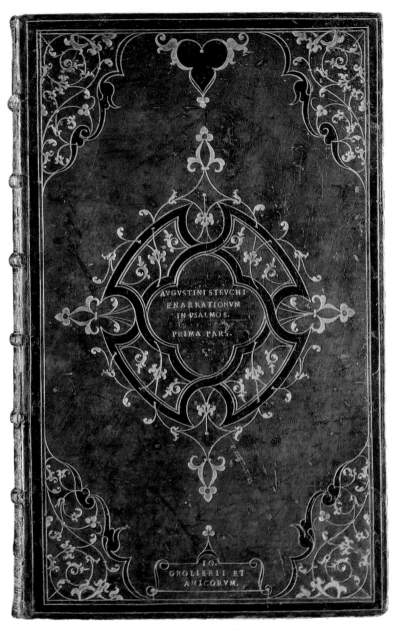

I FRENCH: *c.* 1555–65.
393 × 256 mm.

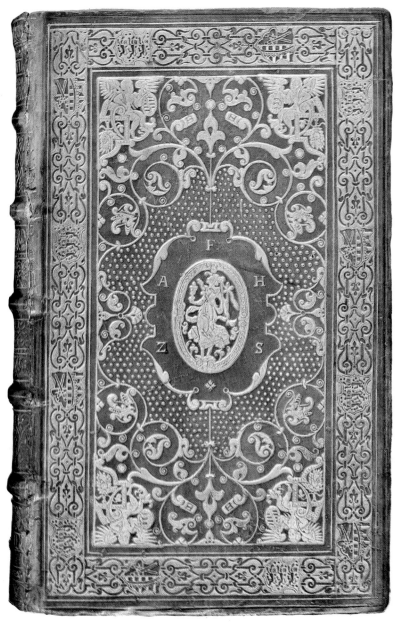

2 GERMAN: 1583.
310 × 192 mm.

Opposite
4 ENGLISH: *c.* 1672.
370 × 235 mm.

6 GERMAN: *c.* 1826.
315 × 250 mm.

7 FRENCH: 1952.
470 × 348 mm.

Opposite
8 ENGLISH: 1980.
350 × 210 mm.

Appendix 1

The technique of bookbinding

THE technical processes of bookbinding, illustrated in this Appendix, are divided into two groups: (1) 'Forwarding' (Plates 1– 8), the processes through which a book passes until it is covered with leather or some other protective material; (2) 'Finishing' (Plates 9–10), the application of lettering, decoration and gilding by tools and stamps. The illustrations show only the principal stages in forwarding and finishing.

For a detailed account of the technique of bookbinding the following books may be consulted.

COCKERELL (D.): *Bookbinding and the care of books.* 4th ed. London, 1939.
DIEHL (E.): *Bookbinding: its background and technique.* Vol. 2. New York, 1946.

1 Sewing The sections are sewn on five raised cords; this is known as flexible style. These cords form the raised bands at the leather covering stage. Sections can also be sewn on recessed cords (where the cord is sewn into the spine via saw cuts) and also on linen tapes.

2 Gluing up the spine Glue is worked into the spine to give strength at the rounding and backing stage. P.V.A. (polyvinyl acetate) can also be used providing a thin coat of paste is applied and allowed to dry first.

3 Backing The spine of the book is formed with the use of a backing hammer to give a semi-elliptic shape; it is then placed between backing boards (usually made of beach and wedge-shaped) and put in a laying press. The sections are hammered over evenly on both sides to form shoulders, to which the cover boards are butted up.

4 Lacing on the boards The cords on which the book is sewn are carefully frayed out, pasted, and passed into and out of the cover boards via pre-punched holes.

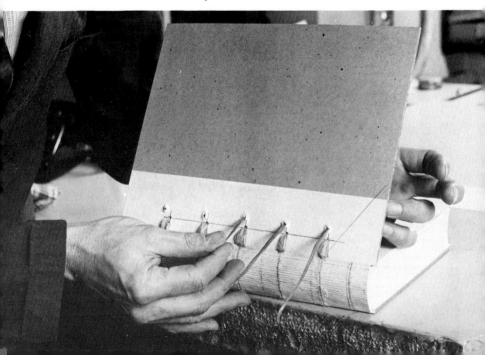

5 Hammering the cords flat The lacing is tapped gently down to grip the cords, excess cord is trimmed. The cords are then hammered flat on a knocking down iron gripped in a laying press. The book is placed in a standing press with tin plates on the inside of the cover boards and metal plates and pressing boards on the outside.

6 Head banding The decorative bands at the head and tail of the spine are sewn with silks over vellum strips, cords or cat gut; they can be of one or more colours and sewn in single or double style.
Head bands are not only decorative but give strength and support at the head and tail of the spine.

7 Leather Paring With the use of a paring knife and spokeshave the leather is pared around the turn-in edges; if the leather is thick a small amount is removed from the spine area.

8 Covering The pared leather is dampened on the grain side, then pasted on the flesh side; when pliable it is drawn over the cover boards and spine. The bands are formed by nipping up the leather over the raised cords with the aid of band nippers.

9 Lettering the spine After lightly polishing the leather the title is impressed on the spine with heated tools. Paste-wash and glaire are then applied, gold leaf is laid over the prepared impressions and the heated tools pressed through the gold leaf; the surplus gold is then removed.

10 Rolling in lines The fillet is used to roll both blind and gold lines along the sides of bindings.

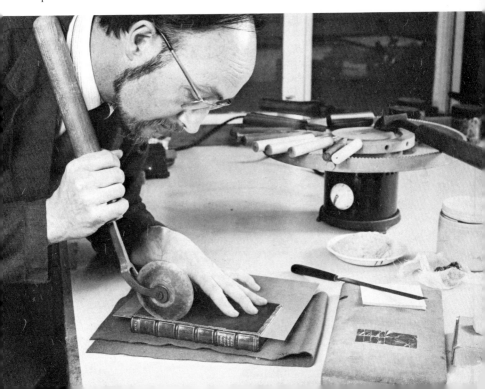

Glossary

BACK: The covered back of the book on which the title is now usually lettered, also called the spine.

BANDS: The cords on which a book is sewn, or the ridges on the back produced by the cords showing through the leather.

BLIND TOOLING: See TOOLING.

CASING: The cover and text of a book made separately and pasted together by means of end-papers.

CUIR CISELÉ: Decoration of the book cover by cutting the design in leather instead of the more normal tooling or stamping.

DOUBLURE: The inside face of the covers, especially when lined with leather and decorated.

END-PAPERS: The leaves added by the binder at the beginning and end of a book.

FILLET: Impressed straight line(s), or the rotating tool used for producing them.

FINISHING: Ornamentation of the book cover by tooling, lettering, etc.

FORWARDING: The processes of binding and covering a book prior to finishing.

GAUFFERING: Decoration of the gilded edges of the book with finishing tools.

MARBLING: The process of colouring the edges and end-papers in conventional imitation of marble.

MOROCCO: Goatskin, originally produced in Morocco, and later imitated in sheep- and lambskin.

PANEL STAMPS: Large metal blocks, cut or engraved with a pictorial or decorative device, usually stamped on the book cover by means of a press.

POINTILLÉ: Dotted decoration in gold.

ROLLS: Cylindrical engraved tools used in gold or blind tooling to produce a repeating design.

SEMIS: An heraldic term signifying a diaper design made by the regular repetition of one or more small tools.

SPINE: See BACK.

TOOLING: Decoration of a binding by means of finishing tools, i.e., rolls or stamps.
  BLIND TOOLING; Tooling without gold.
  GOLD TOOLING: Gold leaf applied by heated tools.

TOOLS: Stamps or dies used in the decoration of a binding, usually impressed by hand.